LEGISLATI

STATUTORY INTERPRETATION: 20 QUESTIONS

by

KENT GREENAWALT

University Professor, Columbia University School of Law

TURNING POINT SERIES®

New York, New York
FOUNDATION PRESS
1999

Cover Drawing: John MacDonald
Williamstown, Massachusetts
Cover Design: Keith Stout
Manhattan, New York

Turning Point Series is a registered trademark
used herein under license.

COPYRIGHT © 1999 By FOUNDATION PRESS
11 Penn Plaza, Tenth Floor
New York, NY 10001
Phone (212) 760–8700
Fax (212) 760–8705

Printed in the United States of America

ISBN 1–56662–784–2

TEXT IS PRINTED ON 10% POST
CONSUMER RECYCLED PAPER

TURNING POINT SERIES

- **CIVIL PROCEDURE: TERRITORIAL JURISDICTION AND VENUE**
  Kevin M. Clermont, Cornell University

- **CIVIL PROCEDURE: CLASS ACTIONS**
  Linda S. Mullenix, University of Texas (Available November 1999)

- **CONSTITUTIONAL LAW: EQUAL PROTECTION**
  Louis Michael Seidman, Georgetown (Available August 2002)

- **LEGISLATION: STATUTORY INTERPRETATION**
  Kent Greenawalt, Columbia University

- **SECURITIES LAW: INSIDER TRADING**
  Stephen M. Bainbridge, UCLA

- **TORT LAW: PROXIMATE CAUSE**
  Joseph A. Page, Georgetown (Available August 2000)

*

To my daughter Sarah,

With love

*

Preface

Having taught statutory interpretation in Columbia's introductory Legal Methods course for some years, and intending in the future to write on the topic, I decided to try to formulate some crucial questions and answer them. I thought this exercise would help give me a clear view about how various issues relate to each other, and about central disputes over how judges interpret statutes. I presented this initial effort in a seminar Jeremy Waldron and I were teaching. Jeremy, along with Peter Strauss, a co-teacher in Legal Methods, encouraged me to think that the effort would have some value for others, including students studying statutory interpretation. Happily, the Board of Editors at Foundation Press regarded my draft as appropriate for its Turning Point Series.

The book as it stands has benefitted tremendously from the help of others. At an early stage, both Jeremy Waldron and Peter Strauss, who for years, along with Arthur Murphy, John Kernochan, and Michael Sovern, and students in Legal Methods, has educated me in this subject, gave me extremely useful comments. Subsequently the manuscript was very carefully reviewed by Daniel Farber, Philip Frickey, John Manning, and David Shapiro. Each gave me many highly detailed and perceptive comments, which exposed weaknesses and caused me to rethink and reformulate positions. I also learned much from faculty discussion groups at Columbia focusing on legal theory and statutory interpretation. The conversation in Professor Waldron's and my 1998 seminar in Theories of Legislation and Legislative Interpretation was also highly fruitful.

I am greatly indebted to Michael Dowdle and Edward Blatnik for their extensive research assistance, which included valuable critical comments as well as discovery and checking of sources. Sally Wrigley has typed successive stages of the manuscript, often under considerable time pressure, with her usual good will and expert hand.

About the Author

Kent Greenawalt is University Professor at Columbia University School of Law. A graduate of Swarthmore College, Oxford University, and Columbia Law School, he was a law clerk to Supreme Court Justice John M. Harlan, and a special assistant at the Agency for International Development, before returning to Columbia to teach in 1965. He was Benjamin N. Cardozo Professor of Jurisprudence before being appointed University Professor. He served as Deputy Solicitor General in 1972–73, is a past president of the American Society for Political and Legal Philosophy, and is a fellow of American Academy of Arts and Sciences and a member of the American Philosophical Society. He is the author of seven books, including Conflicts of Law and Morality (1987), Law and Objectivity (1992), and Fighting Words (1995).

*

TABLE OF CONTENTS

TABLE OF CONTENTS

XIII

TABLE OF CONTENTS

TABLE OF CONTENTS

*

LEGISLATION

STATUTORY INTERPRETATION: 20 QUESTIONS

Twenty Questions

1. Are statutes mandatory or advisory for courts and other official interpreters?

2. Should a statute's content be regarded as determined at the time of enactment, or should events after adoption be relevant for the way language is understood?

3. Should interpretation be entirely, or largely, determined by the meaning of language used in the statute?

4. How, if at all, should evident purposes figure in construction of statutory language?

5. For discerning the meaning of language, should a court adopt the perspective of an ordinary speaker or an expert; and should it focus on the way language was understood at the time of adoption, at the time crucial events occurred, or at the time of interpretation?

6. Should statutory interpretation be guided entirely, or largely, by the mental-state intentions of legislators?

7. If mental-state intentions count, which mental states, actual or hypothetical, matter?

8. If mental-state intentions count, whose mental states matter, and what comparative weight do they have?

9.   How should courts discover relevant mental states?

10.   Should courts make reference to aspects of legislative history, and, if so, on what basis?

11.   How far should interpretations of statutes be influenced by general canons of meaning and interpretation?

12.   How far should interpretations be influenced by principles and policies that bear on the law generally or on particular legal subjects?

13.   In considering whether events after a statute's adoption should matter, how should courts regard the interpretive responsibilities of administrative agencies and executive departments?

14.   How should courts treat changes in the corpus of law and other post-enactment events that might alter the way statutory language could best be interpreted?

15.   Should judges rely self-consciously on their own moral and political judgments?

16.   If judges interpreting statutory language appropriately conceive of its desirable application as shifting over time, should they understand the meaning of a statute itself as changing, or should they regard some desirable present applications as deviating from the statutory meaning; and should they be candid about whatever their understanding is?

17.   Can one answer these sixteen specific questions without analysis that includes evaluative judg-

ments, mainly about political institutions and morality?

18. Can one give answers that are good for all political systems or for all liberal democracies?

19. Will answers that are sound for any one system at one point in time remain sound?

20. To what extent are sound answers tied to existing practice?

CHAPTER I

INTRODUCTION

Understanding relationships is often difficult. Lawyers and students who think about statutory interpretation have trouble keeping in mind how any particular thorny issue relates to other issues. This book sets central practical issues in an overall context. Although less than exhaustive in its treatment of competing positions, the book's comprehensive view assists in clarifying and answering many critical questions about judicial interpretation of statutes.

Statutes are authoritative legal directives. They differ from wills and trusts in that they issue from public authority and are (typically) directed to social problems of general significance. They differ from instructions of one official to another—of the sort Thomas Jefferson as President gave to Meriwether Lewis at the beginning of the Lewis and Clark expedition[1]—in coming from a multi-member body.

Legislative bodies have continuity over time, but their compositions change. A legislature that is seated after an election does not share an identity with its predecessor in the manner of an individual

1. *See* Stephen E. Ambrose, *Undaunted Courage* 116–17 (1996).

1

who has grown older.[2] Most statutes address the behavior of private individuals and organizations or the actions of administrative officials; their final interpretation rests with courts. According to legal doctrine and standard democratic political theory, courts must accept what legislatures have done (unless a statute breaches some higher authoritative law).

This book engages twenty important questions about desirable or appropriate statutory interpretation. One could pose similar descriptive questions about present practice. Although I concentrate primarily on what judges "ought" to do, I comment on the ways in which many of the practices I discuss do fit existing practices; and various ties between actual and desirable practice reduce the gap between "is" and "ought."

Here are the questions: (1) Are statutes mandatory or advisory for courts and other official interpreters? (2) Should a statute's content be regarded as determined at the time of enactment, or should events after adoption be relevant for the way language is understood? (3) Should interpretation be entirely, or largely, determined by the meaning of language used in the statute? (4) How, if at all, should evident purposes figure in construction of statutory language? (5) For discerning the meaning of language, should a court adopt the perspective of

2. However, this "break" in legislative continuity is, for practical purposes, less in cabinet systems when legislatures, with members acting in accord with party discipline, uniformly vote measures proposed by the cabinet, and the party (or parties) already in power wins the election.

an ordinary speaker or an expert; and should it focus on the way language was understood at the time of adoption, at the time crucial events occurred, or at the time of interpretation? (6) Should statutory interpretation be guided entirely, or largely, by the mental-state intentions of legislators? (7) If mental-state intentions count, which mental states, actual or hypothetical, matter? (8) If mental-state intentions count, whose mental states matter, and what comparative weight do they have? (9) How should courts discover relevant mental states? (10) Should courts make reference to aspects of legislative history, and, if so, on what basis? (11) How far should interpretations of statutes be influenced by general canons of meaning and interpretation? (12) How far should interpretations be influenced by principles and policies that bear on the law generally or on particular legal subjects? (13) In considering whether events after a statute's adoption should matter, how should courts regard the interpretive responsibilities of administrative agencies and executive departments? (14) How should courts treat changes in the corpus of law and other post-enactment events that might alter the way statutory language could best be interpreted? (15) Should judges rely self-consciously on their own moral and political judgments? (16) If judges interpreting statutory language appropriately conceive of its desirable application as shifting over time, should they understand the meaning of a statute itself as changing, or should they regard some desirable present applications as deviating from the statutory meaning; and should they be candid about whatever their understanding is? (17) Can one answer these sixteen specific questions without analysis that includes evaluative judgments, mainly about political institutions and morality? (18) Can one give answers that are good for all political systems or for all liberal democracies? (19) Will answers that are sound for any one system at one point in time remain sound? (20) To what extent are sound answers tied to existing practice?

I address each of these twenty questions. Since many questions are closely interrelated, a preliminary answer to an earlier question is vulnerable to being dislodged by a response to a later question. If, for example, someone initially concludes that the mental states of legislators should matter, and later decides that these states cannot be determined in any acceptable way, he would have to revise his initial judgment. Many of my preliminary judgments are provisional in this way.

The questions, as I have here phrased them, are filled with vagueness and ambiguity. My initial aim has been to chart a general map of the territory to be covered, not to attain precision. Subsequent discussion introduces nuance and complexity.

My theoretical ambitions are both modest and broad. I intend the analysis to be easily understandable by lawyers and students who are interested in statutory interpretation but unfamiliar with the increasingly rich literature about interpretation, social choice, and other subjects now relevant to a sophisticated understanding of statutory interpretation. I have tried to provide an account that will stand up to critical analysis, but I do not delve into many complications that are worth exploring. In particular, I do not survey the field of competing theoretical approaches to interpreting statutes and carefully assess the strengths and weaknesses of each approach. This field now includes what is called new "textualism," "intentionalism," "purposivism," "legal process," "pragmatism," and "integrity." I mention these theories in passing as I focus on particular topics; but I believe much can be said about statutory interpretation without resolution of some of the most highly debated questions. Finally, I do not provide the footnotes that would accompany a full scholarly treatment of this topic. So much for modesty.

Breadth is harder to explain. Many reasonable disagreements lead to different opinions about how exactly judges should interpret statutes. Indeed, if one refined any view to its every subtlety, each scholar and each judge would have his or her own singular approach. What I mainly seek to do is to clarify questions and their relationships to each other, and to mark out the boundaries of reasonable disagreement. Two people who agreed with every word of this essay could give substantially different weight to various interpretive guides I claim are relevant, and they could disagree about which theory of interpretation is most attractive. This does not mean I say nothing controversial. I oppose some standard views about statutory interpretation and I show why various approaches are not nearly as simple as they are often taken to be. However, I offer these comments without resolving many arguments about the exact relationships among legislatures, courts, and administrative agencies.

Reflecting what is dominant present practice, I support an approach to statutory interpretation that does not reduce to any simple, single consideration. Original meaning is very important, but some post-enactment events, including prior judicial and administrative decisions, affect what is desirable interpretation. On any tenable theory of interpretation, the meaning of the statutory text to readers matters greatly. In circumstances when apparent meaning may shift from the time of enactment to the time of interpretation, both should ordinarily have some relevance. Some statutes are written for ordinary people, others for experts, and judges should interpret them accordingly. Although plausible arguments can be made for judges disregarding evidence outside the statutory text of what legislators had in mind when they adopted laws, I suggest that reliance on the mental-state intentions of legislators is coherent and does not violate basic premises of liberal democracy. I delve into the intricate questions of which and whose intentions should count. I next suggest that some reliance on what is called "legislative history" is intrinsically appropriate. I recognize, however, that people may reasonably disagree over whether the judicial search for intentions through legislative history is worth the effort. In two chapters, I explain briefly the place of canons of interpretation and broader underlying principles of interpretation. I contend that judges should give some weight to changes in the corpus of law and in the surrounding social environment, but should rarely rely directly on their own moral and political judgment. In the next-to-final chapter, I examine some ways in which judges might understand changes in the applications of statutory provisions.

*

Chapter II

General Theoretical Suppositions

I begin with the last four questions. These concern both how one addresses the other questions and the amount of generality one should expect in answers to those questions.

I. The Need for Judgments of Political Theory at Some Level

The answer to Question 17[3] is that no one can respond to the sixteen specific questions without making evaluative judgments. Someone who initially considers statutory interpretation might hope that certain principles of interpretation will just "fall out" from the nature of language and human communication or from obvious relations of legislatures and courts: "If an elected legislative body adopts a statute, then, *of course*, courts should interpret it in a certain way." One proposition on which scholars now agree is that few of my questions can be answered so simply. Reasonable disagreements about the precise roles of legislatures,

3. "Can one answer these sixteen specific questions without analysis that includes evaluative judgments, mainly about political institutions and morality?"

courts, and administrative agencies, and reasonable disagreements about the qualities of sound law, influence positions on statutory interpretation. One cannot derive all of one's conclusions about the way judges should interpret statutes as logical entailments of "interpretation" or "statutory interpretation"; he or she must argue for most conclusions on the basis of political and legal theory, theory that gives an account of various branches of government and the desirable qualities of law.

People sometimes move, explicitly or implicitly, from the true premise that all approaches rest on political theory to the erroneous proposition that all approaches are equal in the amount of political theory they require of judges. However, a defender of the position that judges should follow original textual meaning might claim that courts should be constrained and that judges are no more competent than others to engage large issues of political theory.[4] He would argue that judges of divergent political persuasions can discern the original meaning of texts without making political judgments of their own.[5] The overarching justification of textual origi-

4. *See* Antonin Scalia, *A Matter of Interpretation: Federal Courts and the Law: An Essay* 44–47 (1996). Bradley C. Karkkainen explains the many ways in which Justice Scalia is less than "pure" about following original meaning in " 'Plain Meaning': Justice Scalia's Jurisprudence of Strict Statutory Construction," 17 HARV. J. OF LAW AND PUBLIC POLICY 401 (1994).

5. Note that I am interested here in the rationale of the position and its ideal operation—not how it does (or would) really work in practice. Perhaps in practice, the relevant understanding at the time of adoption is often so difficult to ascertain that judges must rely on their political beliefs (or something

nalism rests on political theory; but beyond accepting that theory, a judge (so it is claimed) need not undertake political and moral analysis in individual cases. By contrast, the theory that judges should make the best justification they can of statutory language links interpretation in individual cases to political and moral judgment.[6] Two judges who follow this approach may differ about construing a particular text because they disagree about what is politically just. In comparing textual originalism with a best-justification approach, we see that both approaches to statutory interpretation *rest* on political theory, but the latter approach, more than the former, embroils judges in making judgments of political theory that relate to the narrow issues in particular cases.

II. The Relevance of Particular Political Structures

If many conclusions about desirable statutory interpretation rest on political theory, some conclusions, in response to Question 18,[7] will depend on

else). Perhaps in practice, even when a reasonably objective person could discern a relevant understanding, actual judges will pursue political objectives under a thin cover of discovering original meaning. These facts, if true, affect the persuasiveness of any such approach. Here my point is that that approach, in principle, gets judges out of the business of making political judgments in individual cases.

6. *See, e.g.*, Ronald Dworkin, *Law's Empire* 313–54 (1986).

7. "Can one give answers that are good for all political systems or for all liberal democracies?"

the political system in which statutes are being interpreted. This is true, whether the person considering interpretation accepts or rejects the basic political order. I shall concentrate on judges and scholars who accept the systems they analyze, but I first say a few words about the contrasting situation.

Special problems are created when someone considers political institutions she rejects. Suppose an opponent of theocracy evaluates interpretation in a society in which priests compose the legislature and courts. She could ask how judges should interpret if they endorse the system, or how they should interpret if they agree with her that movement away from theocracy is a high priority. In either event, she would probably reach conclusions that would differ from her views about what judges should do in a healthy liberal democracy that she approves.[8] Similar perplexities about perspective arise when one perceives grave injustices that taint otherwise acceptable political features. At the time the Republic of South Africa rested on apartheid as a fundamental political principle, one could contrast statutory interpretation as if one accepted apartheid with statutory interpretation that began from the principle that courts should cabin and undermine that

8. For example, a judge who endorsed the theocracy would probably bring particular spiritual understandings to bear in a way that would be inappropriate in a liberal democracy; a judge who rejected theocracy might adopt interpretive devices that would retard theological ambitions, devices not called for in a liberal democracy.

morally wicked practice.[9]

Henceforth, I shall disregard illegitimate political systems, assuming that a person considering the way judges should interpret within a liberal democracy believes that various forms of liberal democracy are *legitimate enough* for judges to fulfill the potentialities of their systems in their interpretation, not to undermine the systems in whole or in major parts.[10] A political system might be unitary, federal, or multinational. The chief executive might be independent of the legislature (as in the United States) or the executive ministers might be leaders of the legislature (as in the cabinet systems of Great Britain and many other European countries). Elections to the legislature might be by districts choosing single members, or according to some form of proportional representation. Judges might be appointed or elected. The legal system might or might not have a written constitution whose provisions are enforceable by courts. The system might be based on common law or civil law. The courts might develop a great deal of law on their own or, instead, apply provisions adopted by the other branches of government. Rules adopted by the other branches might come primarily from legislatures or from

9. In an address at a memorial ceremony for John Didcott, November 4, 1998, Arthur Chaskalson, the Chief Justice of South Africa's Constitutional Court, describes how Judge Didcott courageously interpreted unjust legislation supporting apartheid to give it as minimal effect as possible. (On file with the author.)

10. One might, nevertheless, think some particular statutes are so unjust that a judge should interpret them in a special way. *See* Ronald Dworkin, *Taking Rights Seriously* 206–222 (1978).

administrative agencies acting under legislative supervision.

We should approach specific questions about interpretation with the caution that sound conclusions about one system may not apply to other legitimate systems. This book focuses primarily on the United States and is restricted to statutory interpretation within common law systems. Given the variant legal traditions of civil law, some conclusions about statutory interpretation in common law jurisdictions may not be transposable to civil law systems. The other major differences in political structure that I have mentioned occur within common law systems. Some of them, at least, bear on the way statutes should be interpreted. Less prominent features may also have an influence. For example, in some countries, including Great Britain, virtually all legislation has taken its final form after passing through a professional bureaucracy whose job is to draft statutes;[11] perhaps courts should approach such statutory texts differently from laws that are "thrown together" without great care.

III. Changes Over Time Within a Legal System

Question 19[12] inquires about changes within one legal system over time. These could affect the best

11. *See, e.g.*, P. S. Atiyah and R. S. Summers, *Form and Substance in Anglo–American Law* 315–18 (1987).

12. "Will answers that are sound for any one system at one point in time remain sound?"

modes of interpretation. If, within one country, haphazard drafting is replaced by a professional office that handles all statutes, that could bear on how judges should approach statutory language. A major development in all complex modern societies is the growth of the administrative state. The amount of legislation has increased tremendously in the twentieth century, and the focus, amount, and quality of legislation have changed drastically from an earlier time. A high proportion of statutes now serve the purpose of authorizing more specific rules and regulations by administrative agencies. It is these administrative rules, rather than the unvarnished terms of the authorizing statutes, that directly regulate individuals and private organizations. Many statutes that authorize administrative action are cast in terms more general than is common for rules that directly prescribe private behavior. In modern administrative states, executive agencies are the original interpreters of many statutes; courts typically review these interpretations and must also interpret agency rules that the statutes authorize.

The book refers to these and other changes in legal systems that people have thought significant. As with a wide variety of practical implications of political philosophy, many recommendations about statutory interpretation should be system-specific and time-specific.

IV. Existing and Desirable Practice

My final broad theoretical point concerns the relation between existing practice and normative recommendation, the subject of Question 20.[13] Law has a certain stickiness. Stability is desirable in a legal system. If a pattern of interpretation can be identified as strongly dominant, that in itself is one reason to continue the pattern. This is not only because judges, like others, do not find it easy to change their behavior. Legislators may have adopted statutes with prevailing interpretive practices in mind, and those who are subject to laws may have similar expectations. Even if no pattern of interpretation is dominant, the attractiveness of a recommended approach increases if the approach already enjoys significant support in practice. Among common law systems, different patterns of interpretation are dominant, and different patterns enjoy significant support; recommendations may vary accordingly.

The desirable inertia of practices of legal interpretation influences how one should conceive any proposals for radical change. Instead of offering recommendations about how judges and other officials should interpret from any moment forward, one might propose a gradual movement toward more desirable practice, in order to allow a smooth bridge from the present to the future.

V. Some Omitted Questions

---

13. "To what extent are sound answers tied to existing practice?"

A number of general theoretical questions about statutory interpretation are not within my twenty questions. Among these are: Is there a difference between judicial discovery (or cognition) in relation to statutes and judicial law creation?; Can interpretation of meaning be distinguished from application of meaning to a particular dispute?; How far do statutes resemble ordinary communications?

Each of these questions, and a number of others, hold substantial interest, but they have more to do with the ways scholars conceptualize what judges and lawyers do than with the practical choices judges and lawyers make. This book concentrates on those practical choices.

A few summary comments should clarify some ways in which what I do discuss relates to these questions that I do not address in any systematic way. In many writings of this century, the distinction between simply "discovering" the law and law-creation figured prominently.[14] More recently the idea that "interpretation" blurs or combines aspects of discovery and creation has taken hold.[15] My own view is the following. When courts assign meaning to statutory words and sentences, one can often speak of pure discovery (when in context the statutory language has only one plausible interpretation) and one can occasionally speak of undoubted

14. See, notably, Reed Dickerson's fine book, *The Interpretation and Application of Statutes* (1975), which presents the distinction as crucial and cites many other scholars of similar view.

15. *See, e.g.*, Ronald Dworkin, *supra* note 6.

creation (when the statutory materials, and other legally relevant factors, are wholly indecisive and the judges deem them to be so); but in most instances when competing arguments have some strength, it is extremely difficult to say in practice and in conceptualization just where discovery gives way to creation. Thus, inquiring what sources judges should use to determine meaning is more profitable than trying to resolve what counts as discovery and what as creation. In contrast to the suggestions of some scholars, I do not suppose that the sources on which judges properly rely depends on whether they are in a zone of discovery or creation.[16]

What of interpretation versus application? On some occasions one can identify a preliminary question about the general meaning of some statutory phrase; once that is answered, judges resolve the question of how the phrase with that meaning applies to the case at hand. But often the issue of general meaning is inextricable from the issue of specific application, and questions about general meaning are almost always formulated with respect to particular circumstances that may or may not be covered by the statutory language.[17] This book dis-

16. For Dickerson, any appropriate use of legislative history depends heavily on this distinction, *see supra* note 14, at 137–97.

17. *Compare* F. deSloovère, "Textual Interpretation of Statutes," 11 N.Y.U.L.Q. REV. 538, 553–58 (1934) (emphasizing distinction between application and interpretation), with H. Jones, "The Plain Meaning Rule and Extrinsic Aids in the Interpretation of Statutes," 1 U. TORONTO L. J. 286, 291 (1947) (contending that separation of interpretation from application is unrealistic).

tinguishes interpretation from application only when that becomes important for a specific topic.

In virtually every chapter, special features of statutes as a form of communication figure importantly. Much of the discussion, therefore, rests on implicit assumptions about how legislation differs from other forms of communication, including informal directives.[18] But I do not try to develop any systematic account of how statutes are similar to, and dissimilar from, other communicative actions.

Another question that I do not engage in this book concerns an important relation between statutes and common law: When a statute definitely does not apply by its own force, how much should its terms influence a court that is developing the common law in a closely related area? I am concerned with how statutes should themselves be understood, not when they should be taken to guide common law development.

VI. Conclusion

I have suggested in this chapter that neither the nature of human communication nor the basic features of liberal democracy yield answers about just how judges and others should interpret statutes. These answers depend largely on complex judgments of political theory. The best methods of statutory interpretation may vary with differences in

18. I treat informal directives in "From the Bottom Up," 82 CORNELL L. REV. 984 (1997).

political institutions. These methods may change even within one legal system as political and legal structures develop. Because stability in law is generally desirable, judges should usually maintain continuity in the methods that they employ to interpret statutes. This consideration ties desirable practice to existing practice in an important respect.

Chapter III

Statutes as Mandatory

Question 1[19] asks whether statutes are mandatory or advisory. This question is not about whether legislators may adopt laws that are designedly advisory for citizens or officials. Some laws are explicitly advisory or are formulated in directive language but without any supporting sanctions. Question 1 is also not about whether courts should take statutes as advice about how to develop related areas of common law that the statutes themselves do not cover. As I indicated in the previous chapter, I do not deal with that problem in this book. My question focuses, rather, on whether courts must accept what a legislature has done, or should regard themselves as free to reject it.

I. Statutes Are Mandatory

In any form of liberal democracy, statutes are mainly mandatory in this sense. The claim, made most prominently by Heidi Hurd,[20] that courts

19. "Are statutes mandatory or advisory for courts and other official interpreters?"

20. Heidi Hurd, "Sovereignty in Silence," 99 YALE L. J. 945, 990–1028 (1990); "Interpreting Authorities," in Andrei Marmor,

should take statutes as a form of advice, not as directives, can be understood in a strong form or in one of two weaker forms. The strong form is that statutes are genuinely advisory and nothing more— that a court may "reject advice" that it deems unfair or unwise, even though what the terms of a statute prescribe is within the constitutional power of government. One weaker form, which I address briefly later in this chapter, is limited to statutory provisions that are thought to offend some fundamental principle of morality or political organization. A second weaker form concerns how courts interpret the terms of a law. Perhaps judges can disregard specific terms in order to satisfy a legislature's overall objectives. Perhaps judges can take apparent legislative conclusions as somewhat less controlling when statutory provisions are old, are based on poor deliberation, or treat subjects, such as trial procedures, about which judges are especially expert. In subsequent chapters, I discuss how more general legislative objectives relate to specific terms of implementation, and how comparative expertness and the passage of time may influence interpretation.

Should a court be able to reject the legislature's advice? Such a claim flies in the face of standard democratic theory. We can imagine societies in which judges are regarded as wise men and women whom less wise legislators may advise but not di-

ed., *Law and Interpretation: Essays in Legal Philosophy* 405–32 (1995). For one opposing view, see Daniel Farber, "Statutory Interpretation and Legislative Supremacy," 78 GEORGETOWN L. J. 281 (1989).

rect.[21] But it is a staple of democratic ideas that an elected legislature has priority determining what shall be law, within any domains not removed from it according to a constitution. One major reason is that, within societies in which desirable policies and principles of justice are contested, resolution of most major political issues by representative bodies is more legitimate than is determination by other agencies of government.

One might argue that in countries where courts can declare legislation unconstitutional, judicial power to disregard unwise statutes is a modest further step. But the argument from a written constitution against such power is stronger. A constitutional marking of some domains as off limits represents a conscious choice to leave remaining domains to legislative authority.

The claim that statutes are advisory might rest upon essentially conceptual analysis or reflect a judgment about the best distribution of authority between legislatures and courts. Professor Hurd suggests that statutes are not genuine communica-

21. Perhaps at some earlier time in history, legislatures were regarded as having very limited authority to set general standards of behavior. *See* Frederich A. von Hayek, *Law, Legislation and Liberty*, 81, 90–91 (1973). If these standards were regarded as matters to be discovered rather than created, judges may not have taken the judgments of legislatures as final. Reed Dickerson marks 1688, the year of the Glorious Revolution, as critical in the development of a notion of legislative supremacy in England, *supra* note 14, at 8, and comments that in the early fourteenth century English statutes had no more authority than case materials. *Id*. at 16.

tions and that this drastically affects how they should be understood. She also suggests that, because people should try to do what is morally right, "[t]he law cannot give us reasons for action."[22] Whether statutes are or are not genuine "communications" does not itself settle the ways in which courts should react to them.[23] And the suggestion that officials should do what is morally right does not determine the ways in which they should regard instructions they receive. An official may think he is justified morally in carrying out some decision that itself is morally undesirable, because a system of government will work most justly overall if officials like him take this approach to their duties. Thus, a jailer is not expected to let free every person he thinks has been jailed unjustly. A jailer does not believe that judges and the warden are giving him "advice" about whom to keep locked up. In a decent legal system, a decision by jailers that orders are not mandatory would be unfortunate.

Conceptual analysis alone cannot establish that judges should take statutes as advisory. Someone supporting that approach must make an argument as to why it would be just or desirable for judges to regard all legislation in this way, even though, were many other officials to adopt this attitude toward instructions they receive, that would be plainly undesirable. Such an argument might build on the

22.   Hurd, Interpreting Authorities, *supra* note 20, at 418.

23.   I respond to this possibility in slightly more detail in Law and Objectivity 245–46 (1992).

expertness, care, and detachment with which judges address issues.

The idea that statutes are merely advisory, in the strong sense of not binding courts, breaks radically with concepts of liberal democracy and the modern traditions of all common law countries, partly exemplified by the carefully formulated structures for lawmaking in those countries. A plausible defense of the position requires a frontal attack on those concepts and traditions. Without trying to imagine such an attack and the responses to it, I conclude that statutes are mandatory, not advisory. Allowing judges a general authority to disregard legislation they think is unwise would give them too much power. Federal judges in the United States are appointed for life. Judges appointed while one party is in power should not be able to defeat major legislative efforts of the opposing party, once that party takes control of the legislative process. Many state court judges in the United States are elected, but most voters know little other than party labels and, occasionally, a few decisions that opponents claim are egregious. Of course, were judges frequently to disregard legislation they deemed unwise, voters might become more attentive to the political proclivities of judges and judicial candidates. But few observers believe that further politicizing elections to state judgeships would improve the quality of the judiciary. A general judicial attitude that statutes are merely advisory would be unhealthy.

II. Rejecting Statutes When Fundamental Principles Are Violated

One cannot so easily dismiss a weaker form of the idea that judges can reject statutes — a form that allows judges to refuse to enforce statutes that violate fundamental principles, even though the statutes do not conflict with a written constitution.[24] A traditional form of this position, which in a time long past enjoyed currency in England and the United States,[25] is that courts should not enforce statutes that offend natural law. A more modern version of the position is that courts should not apply any law that undermines the equality of citizens, say by removing their voting rights.[26] For countries with written constitutions, this subject

24. Another claim that courts should be able to disregard the provisions of legislation concerns provisions that have lain dormant for many years and are not consonant with modern law. *See* Guido Calabresi, *A Common Law for the Age of Statutes* 120–41 (1982). According to this claim, very old, unenforced, statutes may be regarded as no longer in effect. That claim lies on the periphery of subjects I discuss here, and I do not evaluate it.

25. Calder v. Bull, 3 U.S. (3 Dall.) 386, 387–89 (1798) (opinion of Chase, J.). *See* 2 *Kent's Commentaries* 318–19 (6th ed. 1848); 6 N. Dane, *A General Abridgement and Digest of American Law* 429 (1823). *See also* Roscoe Pound, "Common Law and Legislation", in 6 HARV L. REV. 382 (1908).

26. If either version of the position is believed to be sound, it might be claimed further that courts should be able even to declare amendments to a written constitution invalid if they exhibit similar flaws. The Indian Supreme Court has taken this position. *See I. C.* Golak Nath v. Punjab (1967) 2 S.C.R. 762 [India]; Indira Nehru Gandhi v. Raj Narain, A.I.R. 1975 Supreme Court 2299 [India].

lies very close to questions about *how* the constitutions themselves should be interpreted. If courts interpret specific provisions of a constitution broadly, in light of moral and political values, and if they infer implied rights from the structure of the constitution,[27] they will have little occasion to exercise any explicit extra-constitutional power to decline to apply statutes.[28] In rejecting the general notion that statutes are advisory, I leave unresolved the issue of very limited judicial authority to refuse to apply highly unjust or highly undemocratic laws.[29]

27. This is how the Australian Supreme Court has built significant protection for free speech without a free speech guarantee. *See* Nationwide News Pty Ltd. v. Wills (1992) 177 C.L.R. 1; Australian Capital Television Pty Ltd. v. Commonwealth (1992) 177 C.L.R. 106.

28. Even as to constitutional amendments (see *supra* note 26), it may be argued that they offend the spirit of the fundamental core of the constitution.

29. The possibility of recognizing judicial authority to refuse to apply unjust or undemocratic laws lies close to the questions of whether and when a particular injustice warrants judges in subverting a legislature's work by engaging in a kind of official disobedience of law by avoiding the application of some statutory provision. Although I have said that judges should regard legislation as mandatory, I do not suggest that they should *always obey* clear directions. Some outcomes may be so unjust, judges should refuse to comply with statutes. (Some sentences may be so unjust that jailers should release prisoners.) We need not imagine fanciful and controversial examples; the United States once had harsh fugitive-slave laws that were within the constitutional authority of Congress and state legislatures. It would take this book too far afield to consider judicial nullification of law, a subject I address briefly in *Conflicts of Law and Morality* 367–68 (1987). Another related subject I do not treat here is the way a citizen should regard a law he or she believes is unjust. Of course, the citizen will want to avoid unpleasant sanctions; but need she feel under any obligation to comply with the law? One

III. Conclusion

Statutes in modern liberal democracies are mandatory for courts, not advisory. This conclusion does not tell us just how statutes should be understood or how constitutional provisions under which statutes might be held invalid should be construed. This conclusion also does not resolve whether courts should be able to declare invalid statutes that directly offend fundamental political or moral principles.

plausible position on this subject is that citizens do not have a general duty to obey laws. *See id.*

CHAPTER IV

DETERMINATION AT THE TIME OF ENACTMENT?—A PRELIMINARY DISCUSSION

The most fundamental divide in statutory interpretation is whether judges should take the content of statutes as (in some sense) fixed at the time of enactment[30] or as properly evolving over time. Question 2[31] raises this issue.

Whether some version of "fixed at enactment" or "evolving law" is more appealing depends on the persuasiveness of the best version of each approach and on arguments for and against giving weight to various post-enactment events. Because one's choice along this basic divide requires analysis of many specific questions, resolution of this fundamental issue awaits later chapters. This preliminary discussion clarifies what is genuinely in dispute, by noting three matters that are not subject to disagreement.

30. In West Va. Univ. Hosp., Inc., v. Casey, 499 U.S. 83, 101 n.7 (1991), Justice Scalia characterized the "will of Congress" as "a will expressed and fixed in a particular enactment."

31. "Should a statute's content be regarded as determined at the time of enactment, or should events after adoption be relevant for the way language is understood?"

I. Three Clarifications

No one doubts that the meaning of some statutes, as they have in fact been understood judicially, has evolved. People differ over whether judges should self-consciously view statutes as appropriately evolving in this way. They differ over whether a court should acknowledge something like this: "When this law was adopted, perhaps it should have been interpreted so that a party in the position of *A* would have won, but now, twenty years later, it should be interpreted so that Party *A* loses."[32] (Typically courts need not decide that a party like *A* *should* have won twenty years ago, but only that a decision against *A* now does not resolve whether a party like *A* should have won.)

The status of precedents in common law systems reduces the range of disagreement over the legitimacy of judicial reliance on post-enactment events. Even those who assert that the meaning of statutes is fixed at enactment acknowledge that judges should adhere to some precedents about statutory meaning that they now regard as mistaken.[33] Thus, a court might properly follow a precedent that is

32. Part of an "evolving law" approach will be that parties at different times, who resemble each other superficially, are not really similarly situated because the legal or social context has changed. I do not mean in the text to resolve whether parties making apparently similar legal claims at different times are *really* like one another.

33. I refer here to the court that decided the earlier case, as well as any courts subordinate to it.

clearly on point and indicates that *A* should lose, even though the judges believe that the party who was situated as was *A* should have won in the earlier case. Those who believe that the meaning of a statute is fixed at enactment may view "mistaken" precedents more narrowly, and as more easily overruled, than those who favor an "evolving law"; but virtually no one contends that statutory precedents in common law countries should have only the status that the force of their reasoning carries.[34] Mistaken statutory precedents appropriately carry some force.

Finally, any plausible approach to statutory interpretation accords significance to what a statute originally meant. Meaning that evolves must evolve from something. On occasion, judges must interpret statutes soon after enactment, with no intervening events[35] that would affect interpretation. Judges

34. If precedents had *only* this status, they would carry no more force than a professional article asserting the same points that was brought to the attention of the judges. Interestingly, within civil law countries decisions of judges generally have no more authority for subsequent disputes than influential scholarly writings. This difference in approach is one instance of how much can be contingent to particular legal systems. For a thoughtful discussion, see Peter L. Strauss, "The Common Law and Statutes," 70 U. OF COLO. L. REV. 225, 234–36 (1999). Strauss argues that judicial respect for statutory precedent supports a broader approach to interpretation of statutes that does not focus exclusively on pre-enactment events.

35. I mean by an "intervening event" some change in social context, law, or ordinary language that might bear on desirable interpretation. Of course, for any case involving parties in dispute, the "event" of the dispute has occurred, and that dispute may illuminate a legal issue to be resolved. For any case involv-

need standards to decide such cases. Original meaning will also matter when a gap in time separates passage from interpretation. Imagine some ambiguous phrase in a rarely invoked statute. There have been no subsequent interpretations of it and no significant changes in social circumstances. If a court could learn how the now ambiguous term was understood at the time of enactment, that would affect its view of what the statutory language aimed (in some sense) to accomplish. In an article mostly focusing on non-originalism in constitutional interpretation, Paul Brest suggests treating "the text and original history" as having "presumptive weight, but" not as "authoritative or binding."[36] Most proponents of a parallel position in statutory interpretation similarly accord weight to original meaning without treating that meaning as dispositive.

A conclusion in answer to Question 2 that original meaning ordinarily has *some* importance affects how one understands analysis of the more specific questions that follow. When we consider the text as originally understood, or mental-state intentions of legislators, we need to inquire *not only* whether each of these alone or in combination could serve as *the* standard for proper interpretation. If we eventually are persuaded to adopt some "evolving law" view, we still need ask whether the original under-

ing administrative interpretation of a statute, the significant intervening event of that expert construction of meaning will have occurred.

36. Paul Brest, "The Misconceived Quest for Original Understanding," 60 B.U.L. REV 204, 205 (1980).

standing of the text and legislators' intentions figure *among* standards for interpretation.

A corollary follows. It is not only originalists of
various stripes who must engage in the troubling
quest for the right determinant(s) of original meaning; believers in "evolving-law" interpretation must
also address this subject. They cannot content
themselves with knocking down originalist approaches as implausible. They may be able to fudge
their approach to original meaning more than the
statutory originalist; the less the original meaning
matters, the less crucial it will be to have a clear
view of what counts. But any evolutionist who tries
to be systematic will need some basis to resolve
what should constitute relevant statutory meaning
at the time of adoption.[37]

II. Conclusion

___

As actually understood, statutory meaning does
evolve, but there is a serious question as to whether
judges should view it as appropriately evolving.
Judges in common law systems employ at least one
uncontroversial practice of treating statutory provisions differently from the way they might originally

37. I do not mean to suggest that an evolutionist will necessarily have to determine exactly what the original meaning was
in any particular case. If the meaning of a fifty-year-old statute
depends heavily on a fit of the textual language, as presently
understood, with the presently existing corpus of law, an evolutionist can put the statutory text against the existing corpus
without worrying what the text would have been taken to mean
or what the corpus of law looked like at the time of enactment.

have understood them. That practice regards prior judicial interpretations of statutes as precedents. Since "evolving meaning" must evolve from something, and since judicial interpretations sometimes follow closely upon enactment, any theory of statutory interpretation must provide some basis to determine original meaning. It follows that difficulties in that endeavor must perplex evolutionists as well as originalists.

CHAPTER V

TEXTUAL MEANING—HOW CONCLUSIVE?

The textual meaning of statutes is critically important for the way they should be interpreted. This undisputed truth provides a partial answer to Question 3.[38] It remains to ask how textual meaning should be understood and whether textual meaning should sometimes give way to other reasons for reaching a decision. This chapter and the next deal with some basic aspects of textual meaning and with whether apparent meaning should "give way" in some circumstances. Chapter Seven focuses on whose understanding should count, and on whether judges should take as crucial understanding at the time of a statute's adoption or present understanding.

I. Why the Text Matters

No one seriously doubts that interpretation of statutes turns largely on textual meaning. Words in English and other natural languages have conventional meanings. When words are joined together in sentences, these sentences convey meaning to read-

38. "Should interpretation be entirely, or largely, determined by the meaning of language used in the statute?"

ers.[39] This is not to say that words have intrinsic, unchangeable meanings or that sentences can be understood independent of conventions of grammar and interpretation and of various background social understandings. But if a federal statute provides that, for all ordinary income over $80,000 per year, taxpayers will owe thirty-eight percent of that income in taxes, the force of the language is clear for most money over that amount that a taxpayer earns.[40] In countless instances, words of statutes are similarly clear in context.[41] People who are directly subject to the law can be reasonably sure what the words require, and how officials will understand the words. Executive officials and judges realize that they should apply the words according to this ordinary understanding.

Why are statutory words and sentences so important? First, they are what the legislature has voted upon and enacted. They are the standard according

39. I am sidestepping the question of how far words can be understood when they are isolated from the sentences in which they appear. The word "automobile," standing alone, conveys a different sense than the word "asparagus," standing alone; but context in a sentence and paragraph can refine or alter what a term alone conveys.

40. There may, of course, be disputes as to whether certain money a person acquires counts as "ordinary income" or whether the person owes any taxes to the United States government rather than to a foreign one.

41. Quintin Johnstone once wrote, "the degree of ambiguity in most statutes is very slight when applied to most situations. The degree of ambiguity is likely to be substantial only in limited peripheral sets of situations." "An Evaluation of the Rules of Statutory Interpretation," 3 KAN L. REV. 1, 12 (1954).

to which legislators have coordinated their diverse opinions. The legislature's most straightforward authority, often prescribed in a written constitution, is to enact statutory language. A legislature does not have the capacity to implement its will in some other way.[42] All this gives the statutory words a powerful claim to attention and priority. Second, the statutory terms are what is most easily available to members of the public and to those who advise them. Citizens should have some idea what they are expected to do. For ordinary statutory law, the words of statutes are their best guide.[43] Third, statutory language is the most solid indication of what legislators were trying to do. If the mental-state intentions of legislators are important, they are most straightforwardly represented in the statutory words. This does not mean we can move easily from the words of a statute to the dominant intentions of most legislators. Because few legislators review statutory language carefully, and most may have little idea what it contains, the precise terms of any single provision may tell us rather little about what most legislators wanted; but it often remains true that no other guides to intentions are more reliable.

42. In the United States, federal laws must be signed by the president, and state laws by the governor; the procedure for adopting laws thus includes this participation by the executive branch.

43. When statutory language is applied by administrative agencies, the best guide for citizens may be the administrative regulations or interpretations.

II. Evident Purposes and Language

Some crucial issues about textual meaning concern the relationship between the meaning of language and its evident purposes. On some occasions an immediately applicable text will strongly indicate a conclusion, but this conclusion fits badly with the purposes that the language is designed to carry out. On other occasions, one will need to know something about purpose to understand the immediately applicable text. The first kind of situation poses the question of whether purpose should override apparent textual meaning; the second kind of situation raises the question of whether purpose influences initial judgments about meaning. No distinct line demarcates these two sorts of occasions, but understanding the difference between them is critical for an intelligent appraisal of the ways purpose should figure in statutory interpretation.

In this section, instead of assuming that textual meaning and purpose are standards of decision that are in potential opposition, I respond to Question 4's inquiry about the way purpose affects meaning.[44] Statutory language is essentially imperative, a direction about how people should act and about how things should be treated from a legal point of view. One can distinguish the most immediate purpose of imperative language from its ulterior purpose, or chain of purposes. On one side of many

[44]. "How, if at all, should evident purposes figure in construction of statutory language?"

New York City streets are signs that say, "No Parking—Monday and Friday 11:00 a.m.—2:00 p.m." The immediate purpose of this directive is to prohibit parking at the stated times. Any construction of the textual language includes its immediate purpose; that purpose is indissoluble from the directive itself. One who reads the language, and understands its import, simultaneously grasps the immediate purpose. The primary ulterior purpose of the limit on parking is, let us suppose, is to allow street cleaning. There may be other ulterior purposes—such as keeping street cleaners employed and preventing cars from parking at spots for weeks at a time. Does one need to know the ulterior purposes to understand the textual language? "No," although perhaps ulterior purpose could come into play in determining certain applications, such as whether someone can park in a zone in the middle of a hurricane, or at 1:50 p.m. after the street has been cleaned.

On other occasions, ulterior purposes do figure in how one understands language. Gerald Graff offers this example: If *A* says to *B*, "Keep off the grass," he may mean, "Don't step on this lawn," but if he is a drug counselor talking to a former user, he may mean, "Don't smoke marijuana."[45] Communication occurs in social contexts. Background assumptions of various sorts frame meaning. One vital assumption is about what motivates someone to speak. In

45. *See* Gerald Graff, " 'Keep off the Grass,' 'Drop Dead,' and Other Indeterminacies: A Response to Sanford Levinson," 60 Tex. L. Rev. 405, 407–08 (1982).

Graff's example, a listener needs to know the conversation's context in order to know A's meaning; A's evident purpose affects how one understands his words. Context and purpose can lead one to assign a textual meaning that differs radically from an alternative meaning that a sentence would bear if it were viewed in some detached way.

Context and purpose also figure when the problem about meaning does not involve choosing one of two sharply variant alternatives, but filling in at the borders of some very general concepts. Assume that tax rates differ for ordinary income and capital gains, and that people have no doubt as to standard instances of ordinary income and capital gains. However, C has a complicated form of receiving money that seems to be on the edge between the two. Assuming that I.R.S. regulations do not settle the issue, a judge might ask why ordinary income is treated differently from capital gains in order to decide whether the money acquired is one or the other. Here, purposes help to determine coverage at the borders.

Ulterior purposes often influence how people understand imperatives.[46] Philosophers of language debate as to how far one can discern a *literal meaning* for language without introducing context. In the grass example, one might say that literal meaning involves the kind of grass on lawns, and that the marijuana meaning is metaphorical. But on other occasions, neither of two possible meanings is

46. *See* Greenawalt, "The Nature of Rules and the Meaning of Meaning," 72 NOTRE DAME L. REV. 1449, 1462–66 (1997).

more literal than the other. A reference to a woman's "residence" might be to where she is now living or to her permanent home.[47] In any event, the ordinary meaning of the drug counselor's words, spoken in an office, concerns use of marijuana, not lawn grass. If textual meaning is determined by the way people understand sentences, then textual meaning may differ from an acontextual literal meaning.[48] Textual meaning sometimes depends on evident purposes. Thus, purpose may influence the most straightforward textual construction. We cannot completely divorce ordinary meaning from purpose.

If readers understand language in light of their appraisals of writers' purposes, *and* they possess some way to ascertain those purposes accurately, the gap is narrowed between the way readers understand a text, and the way the writer intends it. In the legal context, one may suppose that original reader-understanding is significantly affected by

47. Dickerson, *supra* note 14, at 44–45, uses this example. He helpfully distinguishes ambiguous words from homonyms like "duck," the intended sense of which is almost always revealed in context.

48. The most prominent "textualist" on the U.S. Supreme Court, Antonin Scalia, has been at pains to emphasize that he does not support "strict constructionism, a degraded form of textualism that brings the whole philosophy into disrepute   A text ... should be construed reasonably, to contain all that it fairly means." Scalia, *supra* note 4, at 23. Strict constructionism is not exactly the same as acontextual literalism, but I take Scalia's comments as rejecting literalism as well. Bradley Karkkainen, *supra* note 4, suggests that, in most instances, Justice Scalia has construed statutory language narrowly.

public circumstances that lead to enactment of legislation and reveal the legislators' aims.[49]

How far should judges be influenced by purpose in construing textual language? An opponent of using purpose might argue: "Legislators should try hard to be exact. Statutory drafting has no place for metaphor; and interpreters should not have to grasp underlying purposes to discern ordinary meanings. A legal system works best if interpreters use simple standards to determine meaning. Interpreters should almost always take literal meanings as the textual meaning of statutes."[50] The view that purpose should figure little in the *construction* of meaning fits comfortably with a view that purpose should rarely *override* linguistic meaning. Both views often rest on skepticism about ulterior legislative purposes and how judges may determine them, and on a belief that, even when purposes are placed within the statute itself, direct operative language

49. If one thinks that the most important reader understanding is that of lawyers who undertake some research effort, those readers may be aware of the prior law replaced by a statute and of commission reports urging the need for change. Under such an approach to determining textual meaning, a judge focusing on "reader understanding" may end up consulting many of the same sources as would a judge trying to determine what legislators intended.

50. Frederick Schauer defends such a view in *Playing by the Rules* (1991). His main arguments rest on the nature of language and rules, rather than policy-oriented analyses of legislatures and courts. I indicate my reservations in "The Nature of Rules and the Meaning of Meaning," *supra* note 46, at 1472–77. According to Atiyah and Summers, *supra* note 11, at 100–102, English judges are much less likely to consider purpose than are judges in the United States.

should stand on its own as the main basis for interpretation. An interpreter cannot plausibly disregard purposes altogether, but he can reasonably accord them greater or lesser significance.

III. How Forcefully Does the Text Indicate a Result?—Artificial Quantification

The most serious questions about text versus other possible criteria for decision are whether references to other criteria can sometimes override the apparent textual meaning of the directly applicable provision. Conclusions about textual meaning may be more or less debatable. Sometimes the statutory terms that directly apply will decisively indicate a particular result; at other times, application of the terms is highly arguable. We have linguistic expressions to mark stages along a spectrum. The textual language may be "absolutely clear," "plain," "fairly definite," "arguable but nonetheless determinative," "wholly indecisive."

In the interests of tidy analysis, I quantify the possible decisiveness of textual language in terms of percentages. (I later use the same device for other standards of decision.) Say A is the plaintiff. If the textual language points to A's side one hundred percent, I mean that all reasonable persons (in a minimal sense of "reasonable") would think the specific language clearly indicates a victory for A. If the language points to A's side zero percent, all reasonable persons would suppose the text clearly points to a victory for *A*'s opponent, *B*. If the language points fifty percent toward *A*, then it is completely indecisive between *A* and *B*. If the language points ninety percent toward *A*, most reasonable people would conclude that it strongly supports *A*, but they would see that others could make a contrary argument. If the language points sixty percent toward *A*, most would agree that it favors *A* to some degree, but they would recognize the contrary argument as substantial.

I need to clarify three aspects about this device. First, I am not suggesting a high degree of precision for a subject that does not allow it. The percentages allow an easier grasp of how I regard individual instances of statutory language than would use of verbal phrases like "rather strongly," but the percentages have no magic. Second, they are not wholly reducible to probabilities of some possible fact that may or may not be true.[51] They stand for points on a continuum of strength of argument for one position over another. Third, the numbers of the scale collapse together at least two variables: how many reasonable people would find the argument for *A*'s position persuasive, and how strong they would find his argument to be, in comparison with *B*'s.[52] In

[51]. This sentence would require qualification *if* meaning came down to the intentions of the speaker or to the sense of an ordinary reader, somehow defined. Meaning in statutory law should not be so understood. Insofar as intentions or the responses of ordinary readers do count for interpretation, the percentage figures relate partly to estimations of possible facts.

[52]. Imagine two instances: (1) Everyone thinks *A* has the stronger argument but they think it is a close call; (2) Seventy-

some instances, these variables might deserve separate consideration, but here the scale device mainly reports my own sense of comparative persuasiveness.[53] I assume that, as more people would find *B*'s textual argument to be stronger than *A*'s, more of those who find *A*'s position to be stronger would find the balance of arguments to be close.

In most serious disagreements about statutory interpretations, the textual arguments balance fairly evenly, in the area between thirty and seventy percent on my scale.[54] But occasionally questions arise when the most directly relevant text seems straightforward. I shall begin with those questions.

IV. Possible Reasons to Decide Against Clear Implications of the Directly Applicable Text

Why might a court deviate from the result that a straightforward reading of the directly applicable text strongly indicates? I shall discuss five catego-

five percent of reasonable people think *A* has the stronger argument, they think *B*'s argument is weak; twenty-five percent think *B* has a stronger argument. I might represent both of these situations with a number like sixty-five percent.

53. In theory, I might find *A*'s textual argument to be stronger than *B*'s while recognizing that most relevant reasonable people would disagree. This possibility raises the question how far any person's scale represents his evaluations of the actual weight of arguments, as contrasted with his evaluations of the likely reactions of reasonable people. For purposes of this book, this subtlety is unimportant.

54. I shall later discuss an aspect of criminal statutes that presents an extra complication.

ries: (1) slips that are obvious from a statute's entire text; (2) possible slips that are not obvious from the entire text; (3) applications of provisions that seem at odds with underlying statutory purposes; (4) applications that seem grossly unjust; and (5) applications that conflict with legislative intent independently determined.

A. Slips Obvious From the Text

The first kind of case is simplest. Suppose a city ordinance says, "Homeowners must have snow on their sidewalks forty-eight hours after a snowstorm." This language is immediately suspicious.[55] One could fantasize about imaginary cultures in which people were ordered to keep snow on their sidewalks; that culture is not ours. The provision makes sense only if a "not" is inserted after "must."[56] This conclusion is strengthened if other provisions in the ordinance deal with snow removal. Everyone agrees that judges should sometimes supply omitted words when an omission is obvious given the language of the provision and closely related provisions.[57]

55. Perhaps this text is *so* suspicious, perhaps what it seems to demand is *so* counter to expectations, that one would not even say its language suggests that homeowners must have snow on their sidewalks. One might suggest that an ordinary reader would supply the "not." If so, the literal significance of the terms is opposed to the ordinary understanding of the statutory sentence, for which the reader supplies an obviously missing term.

56. To the same effect, "removed" might follow "sidewalks."

57. *See* Johnson v. United States Gypsum Co., 217 Ark. 264, 229 S.W. 2d 671 (1950), discussed in Henry M. Hart, Jr. and Albert M. Sacks, *The Legal Process: Basic Problems in the*

B. *Possible Slips*

Sometimes a court addresses a strong argument that a word or phrase has been omitted, even though the omission may not be obvious from the provision itself and from surrounding provisions enacted at the same time. Stephen Breyer once discussed a federal statute that forbade possession of "any false, forged, or counterfeit coin, with intent to defraud...."[58] The language seemed to cover false Krugerrands—gold coins that were South African currency. The law had dropped qualifying language that limited the predecessor provision to possession of false United States currency. Congress had kept just such a qualification in a parallel provision forbidding the *making* of counterfeit money. The discrepancy between the language regarding "makes" and that regarding "possesses" was not a sure sign of an unintended omission, but it raised serious doubts (especially since making counterfeit money seems a more serious wrong than possessing it). According to Breyer, the legislative history established clearly that the omission of the qualifying language was a slip. Whether any reference to legislative history was appropriate raises a broad subject

Making and Application of Law 1187–88 (William N. Eskridge, Jr. and Philip Frickey, eds.) (1994). *See also* Scalia, *supra* note 4, at 20–21. Nevertheless, in the particular instance discussed in the text, there may be doubt about imposing minor criminal liability for behavior—failing to remove snow—that statutory terms do not explicitly forbid.

58. Stephen Breyer, "On the Uses of Legislative History in Interpreting Statutes," 65 S. Cal. L. Rev. 845, 850 (1992). His example is drawn from United States v. Falvey, 676 F.2d 871 (1st Cir. 1982).

to which I will turn in due course. But even judges who eschew legislative history should acknowledge that nonobvious slips can be corrected if the actual language corresponds very badly both with that of predecessor provisions and with that of simultaneously enacted, closely related provisions.[59] If judges appropriately correct obvious slips, they also should correct slips that are not immediately obvious but whose presence can be convincingly shown by appropriate techniques of interpretation.

C. *Conflicts With General Purposes*

Evaluation becomes more complicated when no slip has occurred but a particular provision seems to be out of line with the purposes underlying a statute. Let us suppose that a judge ascertains the purpose of a statute in a manner she thinks is appropriate. She looks to the statutory preamble, or she draws from provisions of the statute related to the one being interpreted, or, more controversially, she relies on legislative history. Should the judge give effect to underlying purposes or more specific terms of the applicable provision, if these conflict with each other?

In the famous *Holy Trinity Church* case,[60] the

59. The correspondence must be so bad that it seems highly unlikely the actual language was a result of compromise.

In the counterfeit coin case, correcting the slip entailed *not* punishing someone who was covered by the provision's literal language. Because of notions of fair warning, discussed below, it is much easier to justify corrections that free someone of criminal liability than to justify corrections that impose liability.

60. Church of the Holy Trinity v. United States, 143 U.S. 457 (1892).

U.S. Supreme Court interpreted statutory language barring United States employers from making contracts with aliens living abroad "to perform labor or service of any kind in the United States." The Court conceded that the literal terms of the provision definitely applied to a church's contract with a minister, but it said that the aim of the law was to deal with manual laborers. The act did not apply to bringing "ministers of the Gospel" into the country.[61] Under the Court's analysis, it was not that Congress had failed to use the language it wanted; rather its general language had an unwished-for application. Justice Scalia has recently expressed his strong disagreement with the statutory result in *Holy Trinity Church*; he believes the Court should have stuck with the language Congress had provided.[62]

One can distinguish three arguments against a result like that in *Holy Trinity Church*. The first argument is that judges, using appropriate techniques of interpretation, rarely can identify overriding general purposes that conflict with the language of specific provisions. On this view, the Court in *Holy Trinity Church* lacked any solid basis to

61. One basis for the Court's conclusion was legislative history, but it might have reached the same interpretation without relying on that history. Adrian Vermuele has argued that a more accurate reading on the legislative history supports the textual implication that the statute was not limited to manual laborers. "Legislative History and the Limits of Judicial Competence," 50 STAN L. REV. 1833, 1839–57 (1998).

62. Antonin Scalia, *supra* note 4, at 18–23.

attribute to Congress a purpose that excluded ministerial contracts.

A second argument is still more skeptical about the role of purpose in adjudication. Clear, specific provisions should carry the day, even if they conflict with purposes stated unambiguously in the preamble.[63] Legislators, or draftsmen, are typically more careful about specific coverage than about broad purposes.[64] Moreover, much legislation in the United States results from self-interested pressure and compromise. Perhaps an organization representing American ministers afraid of English competition quietly and successfully lobbied for language in the crucial section that was broader than stated purposes would suggest. No one may have wished publicly to defend coverage of ministerial contracts, but the final language may have been deliberately designed to reach them. If this kind of account of legislation is generally sound, one should not be surprised at disjunctions of stated purposes and specific language; and, arguably, specific language should carry the day.

63. Of course, if more than one purpose is stated, and these are in tension with each other, a provision may further one purpose at the expense of another. I am imagining that the provision conflicts with one stated purpose and does not further any other stated purpose.

64. The extent to which this conclusion is accurate may depend on the care and consistency with which the final language of statutes is adopted. The lesser attention to purpose in England than in the United States (*see supra* note 50) relates partly to the way statutes are drafted in England. *See* Atiyah and Summers, *supra* note 11, at 315–23.

A variation on this argument concerns any debatable interpretation of a statute that would be costly. The legislature may be singlemindedly pursuing a purpose, such as the safety of railroad workers, but its statutory language may reflect a judgment about the limits of reasonable expenses. Thus, in Johnson v. Southern Pacific Co., faced with ambiguous language about whether automatic couplers for one railroad car had to work compatibly with automatic couplers on all other cars, Judge Sanborn urged in the court of appeals[65] that requiring a railroad to have couplers on its cars that would couple automatically with all other cars would be impractical; he implied that the high cost helped explain why Congress had explicitly not imposed such a requirement. No one could doubt that the requirement of universal compatibility in automatic couplers would increase safety to some degree; but this premise does not lead uncontroversially to a conclusion that that interpretation fit best with all purposes of Congress, including its sense of cost.[66]

Whatever the power of these three arguments against purposive interpretation for most cases, none has force for situations in which one cannot imagine that any lawmaker would want the application of the literal language that seems called for. If

65. Johnson v. Southern Pac. Co., 117 F. 462, 469–70 (8th Cir. 1902), *rev'd.*, 196 U.S. 1 (1904). The statute forbade railroads from using cars "not equipped with couplers coupling automatically by impact...."

66. Frank Easterbrook, among others, has emphasized the concern about costs. "Statutes' Domains," 50 U. CHI. L. REV. 533, 541–544 (1983).

a judge is unable to conceive any plausible purpose for applying the language as it literally reads, should he or she refuse to apply it in that way? A light illustration was provided by Lon Fuller who imagined an ordinance forbidding anyone "to sleep in any railway station," applied to a passenger sitting upright in an orderly fashion who has nodded off at 3:00 a.m. waiting for his delayed train.[67]

A more serious example involved a Federal Rule of Evidence, enacted as a statute. Judges were directed to allow evidence of a witness's prior felony convictions before a jury when "the probative value of admitting this evidence outweighs its prejudicial effect to the defendant."[68] Thus, if a defense witness had been convicted of robbery, a judge needed to decide whether the relevance of that conviction, for a jury determining the sincerity of the witness, outweighed the unfairness to the defendant of having the conviction brought to the jury's attention. If the rule were limited to criminal cases, its language would make sense. In criminal trials, one worries about prejudice to defendants more than about prejudice to the state. But for civil cases, no basis exists for treating plaintiffs and defendants differently. Prejudicial effects for plaintiffs (if their witnesses'

67. *See* Lon L. Fuller, "Positivism and Fidelity to Law—A Reply to Professor Hart," 71 HARV L. REV. 630, 664 (1958). I discuss this example in Greenawalt, *supra* note 46, at 1460, 1463–66 (1997). This illustration is powerful so long as one assumes that a neat station is the obvious concern. If protecting passengers against theft and assault were a plausible purpose, application against the sitting passenger could make sense.

68. Green v. Bock Laundry Mach. Co., 490 U.S. 504 (1989).

convictions are revealed) are as troublesome as prejudicial effects for defendants (if their witnesses' convictions are revealed). The U.S. Supreme Court construed the rule to apply only to criminal defendants.[69]

One final argument remains for "sticking with the language," an argument that reaches even senseless applications. It is that judges should not be in the business of deciding whether clear applications make sense, that legislatures will perform more intelligently over time, and that they will interact most effectively with courts if judges generally apply direct statutory language woodenly in accordance with its ordinary linguistic significance.

D. *Conflicts With Justice*

Another situation in which judges may not give terms their straightforward significance is when the result of doing so would yield clear injustice or absurdity.[70] This category slides toward the previous one, because one may say that legislators would not have a purpose to produce absurd or unjust results.[71] When judges draw standards of injustice

69. The court could have cured the anomaly by extending the provision's conditions for exclusion to civil plaintiffs. Its review of legislative history indicated that the focus was on criminal defendants.

70. I am assuming here that this conflict is not great enough to render the provision unconstitutional if it is applied in the "unjust" way.

71. The injustice or absurdity of a result could also be used to argue that a slip had occurred. For example, in United States v. Locke, 471 U.S. 84, 93–94 (1985), it was argued unsuccessfully

from general premises of the legal system or broader social ideas, this ground for disregarding literal language drifts furthest from the legislature's immediate statutory work.[72]

Someone who conceives legislation as appropriately involving a series of ad hoc compromises will be less likely to find injustice than someone who thinks statutory distinctions should be defensible in principle. One interesting case involved a division in the Seventh Circuit[73] (repeated at the Supreme Court)[74] over sentencing for LSD offenses. The literal terms keyed penalties not to the amount of LSD but to the weight of mixtures, such as blotting

that a law requiring renewal of a claim "prior to December 31" should read, "on or prior to December 31." The force of the argument rested on the rarity of using December 30 as the last permissible day to do something, and on the way the language would mislead ordinary people into believing they had until the end of the year. The unfairness of misleading people bolsters an argument that Congress had slipped. Frederick Schauer defends the result in *Locke*, on the basis that a practice of judges correcting language they regarded as mistaken might yield more undesirable results than a practice of following literal language. "The Practice and Problems of Plain Meaning: A Response to Aleinikoff and Shaw," 45 VAND L. REV. 715, 729–31 (1992). Atiyah and Summers, *supra* note 11, at 102, n. 17, remark that "to an English lawyer," the words in *Locke* "could have only one meaning," i.e., the literal meaning that would treat a December 31 filing as too late.

72. One way of understanding the suggestion that legislation is advisory is that judges should disregard specific terms when they think the terms impose substantial injustice (or perhaps are grossly ill conceived in terms of desirable policies).

73. United States v. Marshall, 908 F.2d 1312 (7th Cir.1990) (en banc).

74. Chapman v. United States, 500 U.S. 453 (1991).

paper plus LSD. The consequence of this approach was irrationality, or least disturbing incongruence, among penalties for LSD offenders. A seller of LSD in pure form might be subject to a much lighter sentence than a seller who mixed much less LSD in a heavy carrier. The literal language also provided sentences for many sellers of LSD that were highly severe in comparison with sentences for those convicted in respect to parallel drugs, such as cocaine. These incongruencies reflected no evident legislative objectives.[75] Using a guide of legislative intention, Judge Richard Posner, in dissent, felt much more comfortable "flexibly interpreting" the provisions to have them "make sense" than did the majority.[76] A decision to focus mainly on text does not itself resolve the degree to which judges should qualify specific provisions in light of justice; but most textualists are strongly disinclined to play loose with directly relevant specific provisions of the text.

E. Applications at Odds With Legislative Intentions

Even when judges find no slip in language, no conflict with underlying purpose, and no absurdity or serious injustice, they may determine that the

75. However, I have been impressed by the abilities of first-year students in my Legal Methods class to imagine reasons for distinctions that the Department of Justice apparently failed to offer. The more publicized discrepancy between punishment for possession of "crack" cocaine and possession of cocaine in its powder form was, whatever its wisdom and fairness, undoubtedly by design.

76. U. S. v. Marshall, 908 F.2d at 1335.

drift of the directly applicable language does not conform with the narrow objectives of the legislature in adopting that language. To find such a misfit, judges will have to rely on evidence of intention that is different from evidence that shows how readers (without that evidence) would understand the language that legislators have used. Judges might, for example, have a clear indication in committee reports in both houses of Congress that as to the specific issue raised by the case, legislators meant to accomplish a result different from that which the statutory language itself most naturally suggests.

We can imagine three possible positions about the relevance of such intentions and the evidence supporting them. One position is that statutory language itself counts *only* as it indicates intentions. This position is untenable, both because relevant intentions often do not exist or are not discernible, and because the language that is used to give people instructions matters for its own sake. Another position is that intentions are either an unilluminating fiction or are irrelevant to interpretation. The third position is that clear intentions may be set off against language, with courts resolving in particular cases which of the two will be determinative. I consider the place of intention in later chapters. Here, it is enough to say that, absent injustice or some evident conflict of statutory language with underlying purposes, it would be rare for intentions about a particular issue to be so clear from evidence outside the statutory text that a court would follow them in preference to language that decisively points in a contrary direction.

In the chapter that follows, I turn to situations that more commonly cause trouble: when the language that is directly applicable is unclear in its application.

V. Conclusion

Under any plausible approach to statutory interpretation, the text is very important. It is what legislators have enacted. It is what is most easily available to those who must decide how to act in respect to subjects the statute regulates. It is the most straightforward evidence of what legislators were seeking to accomplish. One should not think of the text as wholly divorced from underlying purposes; people understand the language of communications in relation to the reasons that lie behind the communications.

On some occasions, judges will have reasons to resolve cases contrary to the evident meaning of most directly relevant statutory provisions. They are justified in doing so when there has been a "slip" in the drafting of language, a slip that is obvious or that can be clearly established by appropriate means of interpretation. Somewhat more controversially, judges may also be justified in rejecting a straightforward reading of the text if it is clearly at odds with underlying statutory purpose, is manifestly absurd, or is undoubtedly unjust.

*

CHAPTER VI

TEXTUAL MEANING WHEN THE IMPLICATIONS OF THE DIRECTLY APPLICABLE TEXT ARE NOT CLEAR

In this chapter, I address instances in which reasonable, competing arguments can be made about the apparent meaning of the statutory provision(s) that bears directly on an issue. Let us suppose that the textualist argument for *A* is fifty-five percent, that the textualist argument for *B* is forty-five percent; that is, *A* has a slightly more powerful argument than *B*. When the textual arguments are this close, should they determine the outcome? If not, should they count at all in favor of a judgment for *A*? I need to clear away three preliminary points before reaching the heart of these questions.

I. Clarifications

First, I am here making the simplifying assumption that the textual argument for *A* has the same strength whether one focuses on the time of enactment, the time of the legal transaction, or the time of interpretation. The next chapter discusses divergences in the strength of textual arguments that relate to the passage of time.

Second, in treating fifty percent as the tipping point for the strength of textual (and other) arguments, I am disregarding a significant feature of interpretation of criminal statutes, and some other laws. Whatever the phrasing (two formulations are: "Penal statutes should be strictly construed" and "People should have fair warning that behavior is criminal") there is a "rule of lenity" that criminal provisions ordinarily should not be interpreted to cover behavior unless the text rather clearly covers the behavior. A similar principle applies to certain kinds of civil liabilities about which the government should give "clear notice." If judges were going to interpret a criminal statute solely according to the apparent textual meaning, and A were the prosecutor, he would need an argument more powerful than fifty-five percent to overcome the fair-notice principle. (Perhaps the tipping point would be roughly around seventy percent, though lack of statutory clarity is more acceptable when the law covers actions that everyone would expect to be criminal than when the law reaches actions that people do not regard as intrinsically wrongful.) In our example, neither A nor B has an advantage of the kind a criminal defendant would have; a judge who restricts herself to the linguistic meaning of the operative text and assesses A's textual argument at fifty-five percent would decide for A.

My third (obvious) point is more substantive. Any reasons that are strong enough to override clear textual implications will be strong enough to override a textual argument with a strength of fifty-five percent. For example, a judge who concludes that the interpretation that weakly favors A would be a plain slip will decide in favor of B. For the problem about closely balanced textual arguments to be interesting, we have to assume that B lacks a nontextual argument strong enough to win against a textual argument that strongly favors A.

What reasons might a judge have to decide against A, although A's textual argument is fifty-five percent? She might have weaker arguments within the categories of arguments that could override clear language, or she might have a different kind of argument.

The reasons for overriding very strong textual arguments included slips, great tension with a highly certain statutory purpose, and clear injustice or absurdity. What if A and B have competing arguments about a slip, tension with purpose, or injustice; and B's argument on that point is moderately stronger than A's, say sixty percent to forty percent? Should arguments of this strength be able to outweigh the force of A's textual argument of fifty-five percent?

Judges faced with such arguments could adopt one of three different attitudes. The first would be that, unless another argument is powerfully decisive (say, over ninety percent), judges should stick with the apparent force of the textual language.[77] A second attitude would be to rely wholly on other

77. I am leaving open here whether the textual language would include related provisions or only the most directly applicable language. I discuss this point briefly below.

standards of interpretation once a judge decides
that the natural textual meaning is reasonably arguable. A third attitude would be to treat both the
textual and other arguments as having weight.
Judges would somehow reach conclusions, but without assigning a decisive role to one kind of inquiry
rather than to another.[78]

The serious competitors for judicial attention are
the first and third approaches. Opinions may sometimes suggest that when the language is in doubt,
courts must rely on other criteria of interpretation;
but if one side has a stronger textual argument
than the other, the comparative weight of those
arguments should not vanish altogether.[79] Judges
always (or almost always) have some reason to
interpret statutory language in accord with its apparent meaning. Even if that reason can be outweighed, it should carry the day if the other reasons
themselves point only weakly to a different result.
A's textual argument of fifty-five percent should
often triumph over a purpose or injustice argument

78. Possibly the best approach depends on the kind of legal
problem involved. For example, text might be wholly decisive for
criminal statutes directed at the public; other considerations
might count for determining how an agency should carry forward
authorized technical regulation.

79. Peter Strauss has suggested to me that an administrative
agency, believing that its interpretation will be sustained by
courts because statutory language is indecisive, might well decide
on the basis of policy objectives without regard to whether the
language points weakly in a different direction. Whether Professor Strauss's observation is descriptively accurate, I think that
administrators *should* give some weight to the apparent force of
the language.

of B that is fifty-two percent.[80]

Put abstractly, the third approach, treating various kinds of arguments as having weight, seems messy, but analogous resolutions are common in personal decisions, as well as much moral analysis, political deliberation, and legal thinking. For example, suppose a woman is offered a new job. It will pay less than her present job, will require moving to a location she likes less well than her present home, and will slightly reduce her prospects for advancement; but the job will be more interesting and allow her to contribute to things she cares about. She has to decide whether to accept the job. She cares about salary, place of residence, interest, opportunity to contribute, and likely career advancement, but she has no neat ordering of these factors. Many people believe that sound moral and political thinking should not be reductionist, that various considerations of deontology (right and justice) and consequences figure in a manner that is not reducible to any formula. Judges often resolve common law problems similarly. It would hardly be surprising if

80. In a famous piece of advice about interpretation, Henry M. Hart, Jr. and Albert M. Sacks, *supra* note 57, at 1169, said that judges should interpret statutory words to carry out the statute's purpose "as best it can, making sure" not to give the words "a meaning they will not bear.... " If one takes this passage literally, it sounds as if, when words can bear two different meanings, the one that best accomplishes the purpose should be chosen, even if the words can bear the opposed meaning more comfortably. If Hart and Sacks meant to say that whether words can bear meaning is an either-or question and that it does not matter whether one meaning fits more naturally than another, I disagree.

this approach were appropriate for statutory interpretation.

The first approach also seems initially plausible. Under it, the import of the language would control, barring an overwhelming argument for a contrary interpretation. Why might judges follow this approach? It would be simpler than the third approach and would save time for lawyers and judges; and it *might* increase the occasions on which judges would agree about results. One may doubt whether judges have the capacity to undertake evaluations of various arguments with subtly differing degrees of weight. If judges consider multiple arguments, they have more opportunities to disagree about whether relevant arguments favor one side or the other. And, if they weigh arguments without any applicable formula for comparison, even judges who agree on which arguments favor which parties may not agree on how to "sum up" the final conclusion. One judge may think a particular factor is much more important than her colleagues do. Were judges to stick to one form of argument, say textual meaning, lawyers could focus their endeavors more carefully, and judges who agreed about the direction in which the crucial argument pointed would also agree about the outcome. Further, if judges rarely deviated from the apparent force of the applicable statutory language, legislators might become more careful about the manner in which they adopted statutory formulations.

Whether judges in these circumstances should uniformly follow apparent textual meaning or give weight to other arguments may depend on the kinds of arguments judges are considering. I shall consider these two approaches in connection with possible slips, tension with purpose, and injustice.

II. Reasons to Decide Contrary to Apparent Textual Meaning

A. *Possible Slips*

When the argument that a mistaken omission or inclusion has occurred is only slightly more persuasive than the argument against any slip, the asserted slip will not be obvious from a provision's language, as in our snow-removal example. At most, the literal language will be a little odd. Analysis will then shift to related provisions and overall purposes.[81] Let us assume that the text, as written, weakly supports *A* (fifty-five percent), that *B* has a sixty-percent argument that some important word was omitted; and that with that word added, *B* definitely would win.

I am inclined to think that slip arguments have a special status, not to be lined up as one argument among others. If judges are confident that the legislature has made an inadvertent omission, they should add the necessary language. But if the issue is in serious doubt, judges should accept the lan-

81. A slip argument based on purpose differs from an ordinary purpose argument in that it eventuates in a claim that the court should add or subtract words, not just construe the existing words in one way or another.

guage that the legislature has given them, not substitute other language. After all, it is the legislature's responsibility to adopt statutory language; courts should not alter that language on debatable conjecture. Thus, a closely balanced slip argument favorable to *B* should not outweigh a closely balanced textual argument for *A* that accepts the text as it is written.[82]

B. *Purpose*

The analysis of purpose and justice arguments differs from that of possible slips. Suppose that *A* has a slightly stronger textual argument, fifty-five percent, but *B* has the better argument, sixty percent, based on purpose. Either the relevant purposes are undisputed, and *B* has a stronger argu-

---

82. It might be suggested that slip arguments are often not radically distinct from purpose arguments about how to interpret language. The reading given in *Holy Trinity Church* (see text accompanying *supra* notes 60–62) might be taken as a kind of argument that Congress slipped in failing to make an exception for ministers or all "braintoilers." But the argument did not raise any doubt that the language was what Congress meant to adopt. In contrast, in the counterfeit coin example, see text accompanying *supra* notes 58–59, the court concluded that specific language mistakenly was dropped out in the revision process. In certain cases, it may be harder to say whether a slip is claimed. In Green v. Bock Laundry Mach. Co., 490 U.S. 504 (1989) (see text accompanying *supra* notes 68–69), the Supreme Court construed a rule of evidence cast in terms of the prejudicial effect upon the defendant. The rule made sense only if it was limited to criminal defendants *or* applied to civil plaintiffs as well as civil defendants. If the rulemakers were thinking of criminal defendants and would have added the word "criminal" if the ambiguity of "defendant" had occurred to them, one might call that a kind of "slip," although no intended word was inadvertently omitted.

ment that his reading of the statute will serve them, or *A* and *B* offer variant accounts of relevant purposes, and *B*'s account is more persuasive. I assume for the moment that the way to identify purposes is not in controversy; they are drawn from unimpeachable sources, such as a preamble and other provisions in the same statute.

Should directly applicable textual language control, or should language and purpose both count? I have suggested some reasons why language might control: This would simplify judging, yield more uniform outcomes, and help discipline the legislature in its drafting. Also, skepticism about judicial ability to discern purposes, or about whether one can usefully speak of broad legislative purposes in the face of unprincipled compromises in the legislative process, supports reliance on specific textual language.

In order to evaluate the argument for paying attention to both purpose and language, we must remind ourselves of the two ways in which purpose may figure. Purpose might incline a judge to decide contrary to the ordinary meaning of the directly relevant provision, or it might, as Chapter Five suggests, affect how a judge understands the provision's ordinary meaning. The controversial case of *United Steelworkers of America v. Weber*,[83] widely discussed by scholars of statutory interpretation,[84]

83. 443 U.S. 193 (1979).

84. *See, e.g.*, Ronald Dworkin, "How to Read the Civil Rights Act," in *A Matter of Principle* 317–29 (1985); William Eskridge, *Dynamic Statutory Interpretation* 14–31, 37–44, 203–04, 304–05 affords illustrations. A company with a long history of underemployment of blacks reserved some places in a job training program for black employees. The Supreme Court indicated that the purpose of Title VII of the Civil Rights Act of 1964 was to create job opportunities for blacks.[85] Under two subsections, §§ 703(a)(1)(b) and (d), employers are not allowed to "discriminate" because of race. Although the Court's majority did not make this argument, students have noted that "discriminate" sometimes is used to mean unfavorable treatment for members of oppressed groups. On this understanding, voluntary attempts to assist persons in a minority that has suffered harsh discrimination over long periods of history does not constitute "discrimination" against members of a more privileged majority. Thus, the act's underlying purpose could influence the natural reading of the key word "discriminate," so that when a firm that has long favored whites reserves some places for blacks, it does not "discriminate."

Another subsection of Title VII, § 703(a)(2), says that employers may not "classify (their) employees in any way which would deprive any individual of employment opportunities ... because of such individual's race." Whatever the justification, a white employee who would be chosen, were some places not saved for blacks, seems to be denied an opportu-

(1994); Philip Frickey, "From the Big Sleep to the Big Heat: The Revival of Theory in Statutory Interpretation," 77 MINN L. REV. 241, 245 (1992).

85. This was, itself, a debatable way of putting the main purpose, since one might have concluded that eliminating categorization by race was also a purpose.

nity because of his race.[86] Thus, even if one accepts the Court's rendering of the statute's purpose, a natural reading of *this* statutory language covers classifications on racial grounds that disadvantage whites. Here, I am interested in whether moderately strong purpose arguments should be able to override relatively weak textual arguments.[87]

If judges often consider purpose to some degree in determining the ordinary meaning of language, they may have difficulty saying whether purpose is counting in that way *or* is being used to override ordinary meaning. The line between these two uses of purpose is not always distinct. That is one reason why judges should be able to rely on purpose to override ordinary meaning as well as to discern ordinary meaning. Further, when contentions about the language alone are fairly evenly balanced,

86. William Eskridge, however, who notes the possible ambiguity of "discriminate" in the other subsections, suggests that this subsection may not have been relevant to the training program in *Weber*. "Spinning Legislative Supremacy," 78 GEO L. J. 319, 334–35 (1989).

87. The textual argument for § 703(a)(2) may not be relatively weak. I think a straightforward reading of *that text*, taken by itself, clearly bars preferences that disfavor whites. I discuss below how the language of the two subsections with "discriminate" relates to the language of the subsection without that word.

I do not mean to say that however *Weber* should have been resolved necessarily represents an appropriate approach for more ordinary cases. Peter Strauss has suggested to me that the case is not a good example for ordinary interpretation because such political conflict surrounded the passage of the Civil Rights Act of 1964 and because Congress chose language that was "euphemistic."

judges may disagree about its import; asking them to concentrate on language alone would not yield much gain in uniformity.[88] Just how much weight judges should give purpose in comparison with language should depend on the particular legal problem. When fair notice is of critical importance, specific textual language should be emphasized. A person should not be treated as guilty of a crime if the statutory language does not appear to cover his behavior. If a victory for *A* in accord with text might be at odds with what other closely related provisions do, that is a powerful reason to give weight to overall purpose.[89] A similar judgment might be made if overall purpose seems much more important than the disposition of the particular case.[90] As time passes from enactment, a legislature's broad purposes may have more continuing relevance for unforeseen conditions than the uncertain implications of more specific language.[91] Without proposing any uniform approach to weighing, I

88. This is especially true if we assume that a very strong purpose argument could outweigh even clear language.

89. One might talk here about a general legislative purpose to have consistent applications of related provisions.

90. Andrei Marmor suggests that, from the legislators' point of view, it is always logical to give "further intentions" priority over specific applications, since the applications are means to achieve the ends of the further intentions. Marmor, *Interpretation and Legal Theory* 171 (1992). I explain below why matters are not so simple.

91. William Eskridge, among others, emphasizes the degree to which specific language fits less and less easily to situations as time elapses from an act's passage. *See Dynamic Statutory Interpretation*, *supra* note 84, *passim*.

conclude that debatable purpose arguments should sometimes override debatable arguments about ordinary textual meaning.[92]

C. *Justice*

A judge might conclude that the text gives moderate support to one side but that, on balance, considerations of justice incline to the other side. Thus, a judge might think that the Title VII subsections including the word discriminate are most naturally read to forbid preferences that disadvantage whites, although the contrary reading is also plausible. The same judge might conclude, after weighing all the arguments about the justice of such affirmative action, that justice is served by allowing these preferences, though the aspect of selection by race is troubling from the standpoint of justice. The judge, therefore, believes that textual arguments weakly support the white worker objecting to the training program that has some places reserved for blacks, while justice arguments, on balance, weakly support the company and union defending the program.

The arguments for preferring specific language to arguable considerations of justice are essentially the same as those for preferring specific language to purpose. A further supporting argument is that, unless the injustice of a result is undeniable, judges should not be deciding what outcome is more just

92. However, I should caution the reader that on the basis of anything I have said thus far, the contrary position that text should determine outcome unless a competing purpose argument is overwhelming is also reasonable.

than another. Such decisions are too subjective to be made by officials who are not representative, when they are interpreting standards established by officials who are representative.

The strength of this argument against relying on views about justice depends partly on the bases that judges use to draw their conclusions about justice and on how the claims of justice relate to competing outcomes. When judges draw from the common law tradition or constitutional norms,[93] their bases seem somewhat less subjective than when they decide what is "really" fair or just, according to some moral evaluation. Yet, opponents of reliance on justice can argue that the supposedly objective legal moorings of common law and constitutional law are mostly illusory; that any judge's sense of justice drawn from these traditions is itself largely grounded in her moral evaluations. The concern about subjectivity is somewhat more troublesome if judges disagree about what is just than if they agree about relevant principles of justice but disagree about which of two outcomes will lead to conditions of justice.

A reader's sense of justice figures less in interpretation of ordinary directives than does his sense of the writer's purpose. Further, "justice," viewed alone, is more easily divorceable from the legislative act than is the underlying purpose (although the line between "purpose" and "injustice" blurs if one assumes that legislators would not have a purpose

93. They can draw from constitutional norms without determining that either outcome would be unconstitutional.

to cause injustice). These are reasons why a closely balanced argument about justice may have less power to offset a closely balanced conclusion about language than a similar argument about purpose. It is reasonably arguable that judges should disregard claims about justice if what is "just" is disputed and the claims about justice do not connect to plausible claims about purpose. Nevertheless, I believe that arguments about justice should figure in the mix of relevant arguments, even when no justice argument is overwhelmingly powerful. If these arguments do figure, resolution will depend not only on the persuasiveness of the claim that a result would be unjust, but also on the magnitude of an injustice.

From one controversial perspective, judicial appeals to justice may be on firmer ground than this discussion so far suggests. One may think that courts should operate as a kind of check on legislatures even when they are engaging in statutory interpretation. On this view, judges are much more than faithful agents; their responsibility is partly to restrain the excesses of legislators. Alexander Hamilton put this position boldly in *The Federalist*, No. 78: "the firmness of the judicial magistracy is of vast importance in mitigating the severity and confining the operation of such [unjust and partial] laws."[94] I will later discuss some modern approximations of Hamilton's position; but my comments here about judges relying to some extent on consid-

94. *The Federalist* No. 78, at 521, 528 (Alexander Hamilton) (Jacob E. Cooke ed., 1961).

erations of justice do not depend on a view that countering legislative partiality is a main judicial objective in statutory interpretation.

D. Coherence With Other Law

I have thus far discussed weaker versions of the *kinds of arguments* that might carry the day even against a strong contrary argument about specific language. Are there other qualitatively different arguments that might figure when the language arguments are closely balanced? One possibility is that judges consider which interpretation fits best with the entire corpus of law.

It is uncontroversial that specific statutory language should be interpreted in accord with other provisions of the same statute. A court will want to interpret the various sections of Title VII in a parallel way. Remember that two subsections use the word "discriminate" and another does not.[95] Unless judges can discern a reason for variant coverage under the three subsections, they will interpret all or none of the subsections to allow voluntary affirmative action.[96]

The relevance of parts of the law outside the statute is less obvious. If statutory language clearly

95. See text accompanying *supra* notes 83–87.

96. In this example, the subsection that does not use the word "discriminate" pulls somewhat toward an interpretation of the subsections in which "discriminate" appears that would cover all racial categorization. The subsections with the word "discriminate" may pull somewhat toward a reading of the other subsection that is narrower than forbidding all racial categorization.

breaks with what other statutes and legal rules do, and an interpretation in accord with language is neither seriously unjust nor at odds with statutory purpose, judges should apply the language as written. But when the language is unclear in context, judges properly consider which interpretation coheres best with other law. Such coherence arguments usually link closely to claims of purpose and justice—one assumes that a legislature would want coherent law, and incoherence may signal injustice. But an argument about coherence may have a force that is greater than its relevance as an indicator of legislative purpose and injustice.

Reflection on coherence arguments quickly reveals an issue about when statutory meaning is determined. For one who thinks meaning is determined at enactment, coherence with the law, as it then existed, is what counts. Those who believe that meaning evolves will care about coherence with existing law as well. Chapter Eighteen directly tackles the relevance of changes in law after a statute's enactment.

E. *Intentions*

Another kind of argument that might tell against the debatable implications of statutory language is one to which I referred briefly when discussing clear textual language: The argument is that the specific intentions of the legislators did not include a result weakly indicated by the text. I mean here to refer to arguments about intention other than arguments that the legislators did not want a result that conflicts with their purposes. These arguments about intentions should count only if intentions can be understood in a manner that makes sense and are appropriately discoverable by judges. The status of such arguments, especially those based on legislative history, is now controversial. I discuss them at some length in Chapters Eight through Ten.

III. Conclusion

This chapter has addressed situations in which people can reasonably disagree about the apparent textual meaning of the provisions that are most directly applicable. A judge or other interpreter appropriately gives some weight to what appears to be the most plausible reading, even when that is debatable. The difficult questions are over the weight of other considerations, when these are also arguable. When arguments that a slip has occurred are less than compelling, judges should accept the text as actually adopted. Although one might reasonably believe that in the absence of an overwhelming competing contention about purpose or justice, judges should rely exclusively on the apparent meaning of the text that applies most directly, I have contended that judges sometimes should give weight to conclusions about purpose and justice, even when these are debatable. They also should consider how well a reading of the statutory text fits with the rest of the body of law.

CHAPTER VII

WHOSE UNDERSTANDING OF MEANING?

I. Ordinary Person or Expert?

The first aspect of Question 5[97] about discerning textual meaning is whether the understanding of an ordinary person or an expert should control. That is, should judges take as the meaning of statutory language the reading they think an ordinary person would give, or the reading they think an expert would give? This question is made much more complex because of different kinds of statutes and different degrees of expertness. On the latter subject, is the relevant expert a highly trained lawyer or a specialist in the field of the statute? Is the "ordinary person" an average person or a nonlawyer who is very well educated and has an excellent command of English?

Two observations help cut through these complexities. (1) The kinds of people to whom a statute is mainly addressed should matter greatly. As Jus-

97. "For discerning the meaning of language, should a court adopt the perspective of an ordinary speaker or an expert; and should it focus on the way language was understood at the time of adoption, at the time crucial events occurred, or at the time of interpretation?"

tice Frankfurter once put it, "If a statute is written for ordinary folk, it would be arbitrary not to assume that Congress intended its words to be read with the minds of ordinary men. If they are addressed to specialists, they must be read by judges with the minds of the specialists."[98] (2) Arguments about the understandings of any categories of people whose behavior a statute regulates or who give advice about its meaning should have some relevance.

Many modern statutes are largely addressed at an expert community that is used to technical terms and phrases that would baffle an ordinary person, or to "terms of art," such as "standing," whose technical meaning differs from their common meaning.[99] Suppose a statute is passed regarding the internal operation of atomic energy plants. If some phrase would have a definite meaning to all those who are familiar with atomic energy, courts should give it that construction even if the phrase would have a different meaning, or be meaningless, to those outside the field. On the other hand, a law defining illegal sexual acts should be comprehensi-

98. Felix Frankfurter, "Some Reflections on the Reading of Statutes," 47 COLUM L. REV. 527, 536 (1947).

99. For some statutes, it is debatable whether an ordinary meaning or a specialized legal meaning is intended. *See* Moskal v. United States, 498 U.S. 103 (1990), in which the issue was whether vehicle titles were "falsely made" if they were not forged but contained false information about mileage driven. *See also* Babbitt v. Sweet Home Chapter of Communities for a Great Oregon, 515 U.S. 687 (1995) (on the breadth of the term "takes" as applied to destroying animal habitats).

ble to ordinary people; their understanding should be critical for how the text is understood.

One subtlety concerning the people on whom a statute is mainly focused is whether statutory language applies directly or indirectly to them. Language about sexual crimes applies directly to ordinary people. No officials stand between them and the statute. Much other statutory language regulates private behavior only after more specific rules are adopted by an administrative agency. In these instances of indirect application, people who are subject to regulation are not left to guess about the statutory language; they need respond only after the agency has acted. As a consequence, the understanding of agency experts about statutory language matters more than if the statute applied directly to ordinary citizens. That does not mean that the understanding of those to be regulated is wholly irrelevant. They should be able to hold officials accountable and they deserve some basis to decide whether the agency has acted appropriately. The statutory language remains their primary guide for these purposes.

We need to consider a skeptical argument that the understanding of ordinary people should never count significantly for courts. The argument is that these people don't read statutes, even statutes defining standard crimes. If most people think about what is criminal, they assume that if they observe the conventions of social morality, they will be safe, or they rely on informal "word of mouth," or they consult lawyers. In that event, perhaps courts should forget about the understanding of language of anyone less expert than a lawyer likely to be consulted about a problem. Because competent lawyers do at least minimal research before advising on problems about which they are not certain, the relevant lawyer might be someone who has done such research, discovering, for example, from past cases or other writings, what is included in sexual "crimes against nature."

The position that the understanding of ordinary people should not count is flawed for three important reasons. The first is that even if ordinary people do not directly consult statutes, they should be able to understand the implications of statutory language. After they have violated a law, they should be able to perceive why. Even when people receive legal advice from lawyers, it is preferable for lawyers to be able to point to language that clients understand restricts their behavior, rather than saying, "Well, you might suppose you can do what you want, but according to my specialized expert understanding, you unfortunately cannot." (However, when phrases themselves are so opaque that laypersons would realize they have a special legal or technical meaning, it is less troublesome to suppose that it is up to lawyers to find and reveal that meaning.)

The second reason why the understanding of ordinary people should matter is that lawyers do not have a specialized vocabulary for most subjects. Lawyers may be particularly expert at construing complex forms of language, and they may be ingenious at imagining multiple meanings, but what a typical lawyer makes of some difficult word or phrase is usually not so different from what a well-educated layperson would make of it. Research sometimes reveals special meanings; but often lawyers can give competent advice based on statutory language alone.

The third reason is related to the second. Legislatures are not made up mainly of experts. They are made up of a wide variety of people, with a substantial percentage of lawyers. Unless judges have a basis to suppose otherwise, they should assume that legislators are probably using language in its ordinary sense.

How does a court decide what weight to give various possible understandings? When statutory meaning is doubtful, what the language would mean to an ordinary person, a lawyer giving advice, and an expert in the particular field covered by the statute should usually all have some relevance. If a court decides the statute is mainly for atomic energy experts, their understanding should be given by far the most weight. But it will not necessarily be decisive. Suppose experts disagree about the way a phrase should be understood, and virtually all ordinary people embrace one of those understandings. To quantify, suppose *A* has a fifty-one-percent—forty-nine-percent edge in arguments about expert understanding, and *B* has a ninety-eight-percent—two-percent edge in arguments about ordinary understanding. This decisive imbalance might well tip the scales overall for *B*. Similarly, if a statute is mainly directed at ordinary people, and the argument about ordinary meaning is very close,[100] a clear expert meaning could tip the balance. Usually judges should concentrate on the understanding of members of the *most* relevant community, but occasionally a very powerful argument about understanding among some other group could yield a different final conclusion.[101] Judges rarely admit, or perhaps even perceive, that understandings diverge in this way—they are likely to say that various understandings line up in the same direction—but a careful appraisal of the force of various arguments about understandings might show this kind of weighting.

100. The argument about ordinary meaning could be very close because it is hard to say how most people would understand statutory language in context. It could also be close because most people have some ascertainable view, but the understandings of some groups differ from the understandings of other groups. I do not deal here with the delicate question of what judges should do if they think understandings are divided in this way. The problems are not dissimilar from those that trouble determination of legislative intent when legislators have different intents. The combination problems of legislative intent are treated in Chapter Ten. In an article entitled "Are Mental States Relevant for Statutory and Constitutional Interpretation?" (to be published), I consider analogous problems for constructions of typical readers.

101. One can make a reasonable argument, however, that for statutes that are undoubtedly mainly directed at one community, judges should simplify their task and make a determination based only on the understanding of that community. (Other understandings might still be investigated, but only to shed light on the understanding of the most important community.)

II. Meaning at What Time?

Question 5's second query about textual meaning concerns temporal frame of reference. Should a court ask itself what textual language meant when a statute was adopted, what the language meant when the relevant events took place, or what it *now* means? Because issues about time partly involve relations between statutes and various agencies involved in interpretation, I postpone a number of important issues for later chapters; but I offer some preliminary claims here.

(1) For most modern statutes, and most language in older statutes, time does not pose a practical problem. Judges perceive no shift from how language was understood at adoption to present understanding.

(2) As long as judges regard statutory interpretation as substantially an effort to give effect to what a legislature has done, they should give weight to how language was understood when a statute was adopted. Legislative efforts should not be defeated, just because in the ensuing years some crucial textual term has altered its meaning radically, or changing background conditions have altered what a statutory phrase would be thought to require.

(3) On the other hand, the way a relevant modern audience perceives textual language also makes a difference. Imagine that an ancient statute forbids "crimes against nature," and that when the statute was adopted, that term was widely understood to

encompass all homosexual and heterosexual oral intercourse, as well as all intercourse with animals. Let us suppose that few modern citizens understand the terms to cover heterosexual oral intercourse, many think the phrase covers only intercourse with animals, some think it covers that and homosexual oral intercourse, and others would be completely at sea if one asked them what the phrase means.[102] Because so few people have been charged with the crime in modern times, prosecutions have not kept people informed that, as a legal term, the phrase is very broad. Prosecution to the full extent of the original meaning would be unfair (quite apart from possible constitutional defects, the arbitrariness of excessive prosecutorial discretion, and the moral inappropriateness of restricting sexual acts among adults). Thus, judges have reason to pay attention to modern citizens' conceptions of the crucial terms.

(4) The difference between older and modern understanding narrows, or even collapses, insofar as one assumes that affected people consult lawyers, that a lawyer's research includes discovering original meaning, and that the original meaning should control if lawyers can discern it and communicate it to clients. On these assumptions, the relevant modern understanding would then be that of the well-

---

102.   I am assuming that neither at the time of adoption nor currently has the statutory phrase been taken to mean "those sexual acts believed to be inappropriate for human beings." Were a statute to be so understood, its meaning could remain steady as the acts to which it applied shifted with changes in moral evaluation. Many statutes contain open-ended phrases that invite development in applications over time as conditions and attitudes change.

informed client, and it would follow original meaning. The necessary premises for this view are most plausible when a term has had a clear original meaning that has undergone a radical shift that lawyers may easily identify. Lawyers giving advice are unlikely to pick up more subtle shifts in connotations of words or of background social conditions that might affect how people understand a sentence. We can see that issues about time connect to whether textual meaning should be determined mainly by the understanding of lawyers or unadvised nonlawyers.

(5) Rarely is the time of controlling events a separate, third option. As a theoretical matter, understanding of a statutory text when parties engaged in the behavior that raises a legal issue should matter more than understanding of the text when the court decides. Occasionally, some central event for a lawsuit will have happened decades earlier. A court may have to interpret a corporate charter written fifty years ago against the background of a century-old statute, whose meaning affects the meaning of the charter. In such a case, one might reasonably talk of the meaning of a statutory phrase, when the corporate charter was written, that could vary from both original and modern meaning. But critical events between parties usually occur within a few years prior to a lawsuit. Judges are unlikely to discern a shift in meaning in that space of time. Cases in which textual understanding at the time of triggering events might vary from present understanding are

unusual enough so that I will not consider them further.

As I have suggested about the understanding of ordinary people and experts, arguments about both original and modern understandings should normally carry some weight. We can reach this modest conclusion *without* resolving the basic debates about originalism. A judge who believes that original meaning is of overarching importance decides that *A* has a fifty-one-percent argument on original meaning and a five-percent argument on modern meaning; *B*'s very powerful argument about modern meaning might carry the day, given the close balance in arguments about original meaning. Similarly, a judge who thinks modern meaning is very important, but who regards arguments about it as nearly even, might follow a powerful argument about original meaning.

A strict originalist might initially respond to these conclusions by rejecting the notion that modern meaning is relevant at all, except as it sheds light on probabilities about original meaning. The originalist might claim that the "true meaning" of a communication is the total impact that it makes when it is read in its proper context by a typical member of the audience to whom it is addressed.[103] If it were objected that, for many communications (including much literature), meaning need not be fixed once and for all when language is uttered,[104]

103. *See* Dickerson, *supra* note 14, at 38.

104. Revising a famous statement made by himself and co-author Monroe Beardsley, W. Winsatt, Jr., has written: "The

the originalist might stick to the position that this approach, with its implication that "the critical time is the date of enactment,"[105] remains appropriate for legislation. If *A*'s fifty-one percent argument about original meaning covers everything that bears on original meaning, the text should be read accordingly, even though *B* has an overwhelming argument about modern meaning. Is the originalist's position defensible?

We need to distinguish the originalist's final substantive conclusion from his categorization. First, can judges sensibly treat modern meaning as irrelevant? Unless the originalist offers some account of why modern people affected by a statute should be aware of original meaning,[106] this conclusion is harsh when arguments about original meaning are closely balanced. When fair notice matters, the conclusion is especially harsh. Absent an account of why people now should learn original meaning, one cannot tenably contend that modern understanding of meaning is simply irrelevant, unless one is willing to countenance unjust applications of old statutes.

design or intention of the author is neither available nor desirable as a standard for judging either the meaning or the value of a work of literary art." Winsatt, "Genesis: A Fallacy Revisited," in *The Disciplines of Criticism: Essays in Literary Theory, Interpretation, and History* 193, 222 (1968). I discuss some differences between legal and literary language in *Law and Objectivity*, 73–82 (1992).

105. *See* Dickerson, *supra* note 14 at 126.

106. He might respond, as I have intimated, that they should consult lawyers and that lawyers will discern original meaning reasonably well.

Our originalist might concede the practical point without budging on theory. He might say, "Ordinary meaning of statutory texts is wholly determined by original understanding, but it could be unjust to apply a statute in a manner contrary to a clear, modern understanding.[107] An argument that relies on modern textual understanding is one argument about which applications of a statute are just, and a very powerful argument about justice could win out over a closely balanced argument about ordinary textual meaning. Nevertheless, we should understand what has happened as considerations of justice outweighing probable meaning."

Though I have shown why a modern meaning at odds with probable original meaning should sometimes be relevant to a final decision, I have not yet provided good reasons for rejecting a conceptualization that modern understanding matters only for justice. My reasons for conceiving the treatment of modern meaning and original meaning as taking place within the rubric of textual meaning itself follow from my rejection of originalism in favor of an approach that accepts evolution in meaning. I defend this position in Chapters Fifteen through Nineteen.

107. I am assuming here that there is no broad defense of justification or excuse to violation of the statutory provision, that the issue is how the provision itself is to be applied. If there is a general defense of some sort, the interpreter may say that the provision itself was violated, but that the person who did so was justified or excused because of the modern meaning of the language.

III. Conclusion

In inquiries about textual meaning, should the understanding of an ordinary person, an expert in the field, or a lawyer control? That depends primarily on the nature of a statute and its main intended audience. If there is a difference in the understanding of people at the time of enactment and at the time of interpretation, both understandings should be relevant. Just how much each understanding should count is debatable and will depend on the particular legal issue involved.

*

CHAPTER VIII

THE RELEVANCE OF THE MENTAL–STATE INTENTIONS OF THE ADOPTERS

I. What Amounts to Reliance on Mental–State Intentions

Few subjects about legislative interpretation are as puzzling as the concept of legislative intent. Courts often say their aim is to discern legislative intent, but exactly what judges mean by this is often difficult to ascertain from their opinions. Insofar as they do have a definite understanding, judges mean different things. They may mean what actual legislators had in mind, or they may regard legislative intent as a fiction,[108] or as the conclusion of a process of interpretation that focuses on the language of the operative section and surrounding provisions, purposes contained in the legislation itself, and perhaps other factors. A judge might ask, for example, "Taking all these things into account, what would a reasonable legislator (or a typical reader of the statutory language) understand the force of the language to be?" or "How should this

---

108. Max Radin wrote of "the intent of the legislator" as a "transparent and absurd fiction." "Statutory Interpretation," 43 HARV. L. REV. 863, 870 (1930).

language best be construed?'' Her answer to either question might be phrased as the ''legislative intent,'' despite the absence of any reference to the mental states of legislators who enacted the statute.

Oliver Wendell Holmes, Jr. wrote that, in interpreting legal documents (including statutes), ''we ask, not what this man meant, but what those words would mean in the mouth of a normal speaker of English, using them in the circumstances in which they were used.''[109] In the railroad-safety case I have already mentioned, Judge Sanborn put it this way: ''The primary rule for the interpretation of a statute ... is to ascertain, if possible, ... the intention which the legislative body ... [has] expressed therein. But it is the intention expressed in the law ... and that only, that the courts may give effect to.''[110] Nearly a century later, Justice Scalia commented, ''We look for a sort of 'objectified' intent—the intent that a reasonable person would gather from the text of the law, placed alongside the remainder of the *corpus juris*.''[111] We may speak of a fully objective legislative intent as one that does not depend on the mental states of any particular legislators. It may be assessed mainly in terms of how a reasonable reader would understand the language the legislature has used.

109. Oliver W. Holmes, Jr., ''The Theory of Legal Interpretation,'' 12 HARV L. REV. 417–18 (1899).

110. Johnson v. Southern Pac. Co., 117 F. 462, 465 (8th Cir. 1902), *rev'd.*, 196 U.S. 1 (1904).

111. Scalia, *supra* note 4, at 17.

An alternative approach is to conceive the actual or probable intentions of legislators as making a significant difference. These intentions would function like those ascribed to individual action. People sometimes misspeak. Their intention is to say one thing and accomplish one purpose, but their language suggests something else. When either a door or window might reasonably be shut, *A* says, "Shut the door"; but he has slipped; his *intention* is to have the window shut. In other situations, *A* may utter the words he intends; but he may intend the words to cover circumstances somewhat different from those that an ordinary listener would suppose. In short, a speaker's actual intentions may not fit what a listener who made no reference to his intentions would conclude from his language. Some judges and scholars believe that the actual intentions of legislators should matter for interpretation. A proponent of this position might repeat the words of James Landis, who once wrote, "The tenure of the legislator, his parochial interests, his opportunities for extended investigation and debate, his unlimited powers of choice between competing devices, the numbers that he must convince, and the ephemerality of his conclusions, all make for emphasizing the importance of his intent."[112]

The question I address here, Question 6,[113] asks

112. James Landis, "A Note on 'Statutory Interpretation,' " 43 HARV L. REV. 886, 888 (1930). It is arguable just how far Landis's own view of legislative intent rested on the actual mental intentions of legislators.

113. "Should statutory interpretation be guided entirely, or largely, by the mental-state intentions of legislators?"

whether the mental-state intentions of legislators (and possibly others) should figure in statutory interpretation. These intentions might involve purposes that statutes are designed to achieve or understandings about the coverage of specific provisions, or both. The subject of legislative intent links closely to use of legislative history. Many of those who believe the intentions of legislators should count tend to justify judicial use of legislative history to help discern legislative intent. Most opponents of using legislative history do not think judges should consider mental-state intentions. But it helps analytically to distinguish legislators' intentions from legislative history. Some argue that the use of legislative history is justified for reasons that do not involve mental-state intentions; and one might believe that intentions are a useful aid to interpretation without thinking that judges should look at legislative history. In this section, I concentrate on intentions, apart from issues of legislative history.

As we approach the problem of legislative intent, it helps to keep in mind different bases on which someone might reject the idea of judges trying to discern the subjective mental states of legislators: general communication theory; redundancy; constitutional authority; incoherence; and impracticality. These five bases are distinguishable, but arguments based on them often combine.

When people have focused on the meanings of linguistic utterances, they have tended to emphasize the speaker's intent or the listener's reasonable reaction. Thus, a famous nineteenth-century account of political and legal interpretation says, "Interpretation is the act of finding out the true sense of any form of words: that is the sense which their author intended to convey, and of enabling others to derive from them the same idea which the author intended to convey."[114] An important modern work on statutory interpretation comments, "The reach of a statute should be measured ... by the range of subjective connotations that it establishes in the mind of the typical reader."[115] What can one say about a writer-speaker and a reader-listener in general? If ordinary communication is successful,[116] the reader will substantially grasp the writer's meaning. Writer and reader understanding usually overlap to a very high degree. For instances of divergence, no reason having to do with human communication in general supports privileging the writer's understanding over the reader's, or vice versa. One can decide whose understanding counts the most only by knowing more about social context, in particular, the relation of writer and reader and the purpose of the communication. For statutory interpretation, we need to move beyond some broad

114. Francis Lieber, *Legal and Political Hermeneutics* 23 (1839).

115. Dickerson, *supra* note 14, at 23. For his conclusion, Dickerson relies substantially upon political structures and legal processes, not solely the general nature of communication and interpretation.

116. By "ordinary communication," I mean here to exclude poetry and other literature that may be designed to stimulate ideas in readers that the writer does not have.

philosophy of communication to inquiries about political institutions.

The problem about possible redundancy involves the sources on which judges rely in discerning statutory meaning. A reference to likely intentions of legislators could make a difference only if an investigation of intentions might point to a reading that varies from the reading suggested by other relevant standards. Not every reference to intentions would meet this condition. Suppose a judge believes that the only criterion of proper interpretation is what a typical reader would understand by the textual language, in light of purposes that are stated in the statute itself or evident from surrounding provisions. The judge could carry out this exercise without any attention to legislators' mental states. However, she might think she could helpfully refer to likely intentions as a reader would understand them and she might assume that these "likely intentions" could reasonably be cast as the probable mental-state intentions of many legislators. Our judge might engage in talk about probable mental-state intentions while she defends an approach to interpretation in which these would not figure independently.

Attention to the mental states of legislators figures independently for a judge who treats the history of prior legislation and social conditions as important because they reveal what legislators were consciously aiming to do. The judge is open to assigning these matters a weight beyond the extent to which they would color an ordinary reader's understanding of the statutory language. She looks at sources of evidence about mental-state intentions that could yield a different interpretation of a text than she would reach by other means. In all that follows, I discuss reference to intentions that might make a difference in interpretation, not merely conclusory, intentionalist language tacked onto nonintentionalist standards of interpretation.[117]

II. Relevance and Coherence

To understand arguments about legislative intentions, we need to ask what the intentions might be relevant to, whether the concept of legislative intentions is coherent, and whether intentions should reasonably figure in interpretation if judges can ascertain the crucial mental states with some confidence. Even if one concludes, as I shall, that the concept is coherent and that mental-state intentions, on a preliminary view, reasonably figure in interpretation, that alone does not justify their use by judges. One must also believe that, frequently enough, they are reasonably ascertainable and that

117. This classifactory division is troublesome when judges interpreting statutes consult what particular legislators have said about a prospective law, but they (or others) claim that they are not referring to mental-state intentions. They may say that judges appropriately understand what mischief legislators were addressing or that conventional standards of interpretation make legislative statements part of what a reasonable reader would understand by statutory language. At the edges, the gap between an approach that inquires about genuine mental-state intentions and one that does not becomes rather thin. See Greenawalt, *supra* note 100, for a fuller exploration.

judicial endeavors to discover them will enrich the process of interpretation and not undercut legislative responsibility. These are subjects for Chapters Eleven and Twelve.

Mental-state intentions could be relevant to the specific import of a particular section or to a legislature's underlying purposes,[118] what Andrei Marmor calls "further intentions."[119] Suppose a parent about to go out says to a teenage child, "Go to bed at 11:00 when the 9:00 movie is over." Unbeknownst to the parent, the 9:00 movie on this night lasts until 12:30 a.m. On its face, the instruction is ambiguous about whether the child should go to bed at 11:00. But the parent might say the next day, "I intended that you go to bed at 11:00 [specific intent]; the end of the movie was incidental; my reason was that you need to get enough sleep for school [purpose]." If mental-state intentions matter at all, they could count for directly assigning specific meaning to language or for discerning broader purposes, or both.

Is the concept of legislative intentions coherent? At first glance, the soundness of a concept of legislative intentions may seem tied to whether one can speak of the intentions of a group in this context.[120] Phrases like "the intent of the legislature" serve to reinforce this apparent connection. I shall begin

118. *See* Hart and Sacks, *supra* note 57, at 1228–30.

119. Andrei Marmor, *Interpretation and Legal Theory* 166 (1992). Usually, but not always, the further intention involves some broader objective than the immediate aim.

120. Jeremy Waldron dislodged me from this conclusion.

with a brief treatment of group intent and then explain why the real issues about statutory interpretation do not rest on whether "the legislature" has an intent.

In some circumstances, one can undoubtedly speak of the intent of a group. If all, or virtually all, members of the group have the same specific intention, the intention is relevant to their participation together, and the members know the intention is shared, we can sensibly say that that is the group's intent.[121] If, for example, the father says to the teenage daughter in the presence of the mother, "We agree that you should go to bed.... ," and the mother and father have the same view about their child's bedtime, we can comfortably speak of the mental-state intention of the parents. What is true about a group of two is possibly true about a much larger group. Any suggestion that one can never speak of group intentions is fallacious.

Whether one can speak of the intentions of a group in certain other circumstances is controversial. What of an intention that is explicitly shared but has no bearing on the reason the group is a group? One would not say Congress had an intent to see the movie *Titanic*, even if each member of Congress revealed that he or she planned to see the movie within the next week. What of an intention that members have in common that relates to the group but is not revealed? Actual communication

121. Marmor writes of "shared intentions," *supra* note 119, at 162. He also notes that sometimes there are established conventions as to which members' intentions represent those of a group. *Id.* at 159.

among members may not be a crucial condition of a group intention, but perhaps the members need to assume that others share their intentions.

If one proceeded down the path of trying to resolve the precise limits of group intentions, one could then apply the results of that inquiry to the work of legislative bodies. But the crucial question is not whether the mental states of members of a legislature will often amount to a "group intention." It is whether judges appropriately take into account the mental states of legislators when judges interpret the statutory output of legislators. This question is best faced directly, not in terms of whether the mental states of members amount to some kind of "group intention" within ordinary understandings of group intention.

Should mental-state intentions figure in interpretation? If they are confidently known, there are powerful reasons why they should definitely figure on at least some occasions.

I want to draw three distinctions: between situations in which the listener aims to carry out the aims of the speaker, and those in which the listener is having some range of choice restricted; between situations in which the speaker is regarded as more expert than the listener, and those in which he is not; and between initial interpretation by an addressee, and review of the actions of the addressee by someone else.[122]

122. I explore these matters with regard to informal instructions in "From the Bottom Up," *supra* note 18, at 1017, 1020–22, 1024–26.

The last distinction is the most straightforward. Contrary to her parents' intention, the daughter has stayed up until 12:30 a.m. Having intended the earlier bedtime, her parents consider disciplinary action.[123] The daughter responds: (1) "I thought the end of the movie counted"; or (2) "I wasn't sure what mattered most to you, so I used my best judgment." The parents might suspect that their child guessed more about their wishes than she admits, but they might not be sure. When someone (whether the original speaker or another person) reviews the behavior of the original listener and decides whether to impose disciplinary consequences, he can fairly rely on the speaker's actual mental-state intentions to the listener's detriment only if he thinks the listener was or should have been aware of those intentions (or had strong independent reasons for acting in accord with what those intentions were).[124] Matters are more complicated if a reviewer must decide which of the two

123. Of course, if their original intention had been to allow the child to stay up until the end of the movie, whenever that was, they could not reasonably consider discipline. In this instance, specific intent might be relevant to conclude that no wrong had been done.

124. Suppose instructions are ambiguous about whether they proscribe behavior, and the behavior is seriously wrongful. One might think someone engaging in the behavior should not be disciplined if the person issuing the instructions did not intend to cover the behavior. But if the instructor *did* intend to cover the behavior, discipline might seem appropriate whether or not the subject of the instructions should have gauged the intentions, on the ground that she should have realized the behavior was wrong and should have refrained if there was any possibility of coverage.

competing parties will receive a benefit, or shoulder a burden, but the reviewer should still consider what the parties knew or should have known about the speaker's intentions.

The other two distinctions are more elusive. Suppose that a boss gives an instruction to her secretary. Both she and the secretary assume that (within the domain of the instruction) the secretary's job is to carry out the boss's purposes. That is, the secretary has no proper interest of her own, distinguished from that of the boss. If the secretary is confident about the boss's mental-state intentions, she will try to fulfill them. When President Jefferson gave instructions to his former secretary, Meriwether Lewis, about the latter's expedition to the West, Lewis may have regarded those instructions similarly. This is the basic model of instructions from principal to agent in which the agent should care dominantly about the principal's intentions.

One might imagine that the relationship should be the same between Congress and an administrative agency. If Congress has expressed a definite will in a statute, the agency should try to carry it out. Judge Posner once suggested a military comparison for courts construing legislation. He wrote that, when communication has broken down, "The platoon commander will ask himself, if he is a responsible officer: what would the company commander have wanted me to do if communication failed?"[125]

125. Richard A. Posner, "Legal Formalism, Legal Realism, and the Interpretation of Statutes and the Constitution," 37 CASE W. RES L. REV. 179, 190 (1986–87).

Sometimes instructions mainly restrict. An addressee is free to do what he wants, except as limited by the person issuing the instruction. The teenage daughter may resent her parents saying anything about her bedtime; she may think she should be able to stay up as late as she wants, recognizing, however, that she has a responsibility to conform to any specific parental instructions. Or, suppose the boss gives directions about what secretaries should wear to work. The recipients of such instructions may think they are entitled to rely on the reasonable interpretation most favorable to their interests, even if they suspect that that interpretation does not fit the mental-state intentions of the speaker. Statutes that primarily restrict freedom of behavior present an obvious analogue. For these situations, relations between the speaker and listener make it arguable to what extent the speaker's intentions count, even if the listener can infer them. Thus, mental-state intentions might be more relevant for some laws than for others.

The third distinction concerns the basis for the speaker's instruction. If the speaker is more expert than the listener, and is known to be so by the listener, the listener has a reason to interpret ambiguous or vague instructions according to the speaker's intent. This is one reason why a nurse will carry out a doctor's ambiguous direction about medication in accordance with her understanding of the doctor's wishes. Building on Joseph Raz's conception of authority—that the person in authority knows better what should be done than the person subject to authority—Andrei Marmor has argued that, when legislative authority rests on this basis, the presence of specific intentions among legislators "provides the judge with reason to decide a legal dispute in accord with the legislative intent."[126] On other occasions, the authority of the legislature may lie in its ability to coordinate, not in its wisdom. For these circumstances, Marmor finds no reason to defer to intentions about matters that are not resolved by the language the legislature has used to perform the function of coordination.[127] If the text itself does not resolve an issue, judges have no good reason to repair to legislative intentions rather than developing another resolution.

On still other occasions, which Marmor does not discuss, the legislature may dictate to an agency that is both more expert and fully able to perform coordination on its own. In these circumstances, the authority of the legislature lies in its political representativeness and on its place in a total political structure that deserves support. Since Marmor finds no reason to follow legislators' intentions when the legislature's only advantage is its better position to coordinate, he would presumably not think judges should follow intentions when the legislature possesses neither expertness nor superior ability to coordinate. I believe that Marmor is on strong ground in suggesting that expertness makes deference to intentions especially appropriate, but the superior political position of legislatures affords

126.   Marmor, *supra* note 119, at 156.
127.   *Id*. at 179.

a separate, more general, reason to follow intentions.

III.   Issues of Authority and Value

It is time to face a rejoinder to arguments for reliance on the mental states of legislators: namely that the authority of legislators is limited to their enactment of the language of statutes; this authority does not license legislators to control by their intentions. The United States Constitution prescribes exactly the way legislation is to be enacted. The enacted legislation consists of adopted words.[128] Congress exceeds its authority if it controls behavior by intentions that are not accurately reflected in the words it has enacted.

One way of understanding such an argument is as a general one about the way the language of authoritative directives should be interpreted. The general argument would be that, if one person is bound only to follow the instructions (not the uncommunicated wishes) of another, the latter's subjective wishes about the way his instructions should be taken are also irrelevant. To test this thesis, suppose *B* agrees to tutor *A*'s children. *A* and *B* agree that *B* can exercise his own judgment about the children's education *unless A* has given him explicit instructions about what to do. *A*, before setting off on a long trek in the Himalayas, writes *B* a letter saying, "Please teach the children about religion this sum-

128.   *See* Dickerson, *supra* note 14, at 9–10.

mer." *B* initially concludes that spending some modest amount of time on the influence and importance of major religions will satisfy *A*'s instructions. But a conversation with a friend of *A*'s, one who had who talked to *A* about her aspirations, leads *B* to believe that *A* had intended *B* to spend most of his summer instructional time on religion and to teach Christian doctrines in some depth. *B* further comes to believe that *A* had thought her directive had effectively conveyed that. If *B* had received no relevant instructions whatsoever, his learning about *A*'s hopes would not impose a responsibility on him to spend time on religion, since his agreement with *A* is that he can use his own judgment unless otherwise instructed. Does *A*'s failure to express her wishes clearly mean that the revealed wishes are irrelevant to *B*'s responsibilities? Or, given *A*'s directive, and her intended meaning for that directive, does *B* have a responsibility to carry out the intended meaning though he believes that meaning varies from what a typical reader of the directive alone would conclude? We cannot answer these questions without knowing more about the relations between *A* and *B*. Depending on how they conceive their respective responsibilities about the children's education, *B* might or might not believe he has a duty to do what he now thinks *A* had meant to accomplish by her instruction.

Our inability to reach a confident answer about *B*'s duty itself provides an important answer to the more general question about the possible significance of intentions of those issuing instructions. We can imagine circumstances in which one person can direct the actions of another only by instructions, but the receiver of the instructions, when issued, should fulfill them according to the writer's known intent, even if that intent deviates from a typical reader's understanding of the instructions. The mere specification as to the manner legislation is to be made does not itself settle whether the intent of legislators should figure in interpretation of what the legislators have enacted.

Jeremy Waldron offers a powerful challenge to any reliance on legislative intentions that focuses more narrowly on the characteristics of legislation and legislative bodies.[129] In the form in which he makes the argument, Waldron rules out any reference to intentions. The argument, which partly echoes comments of Frank Easterbrook[130] and others,[131] proceeds as if the conclusion follows from an understanding of the nature of modern legislatures. Waldron gives us excellent reasons to be extremely cautious, both about moving from models of individual authority and intentions to the authority of legislatures and about judicial reliance on inten-

129. *See* Jeremy Waldron, "Legislators' Intentions and Unintentional Legislation," in Andrei Marmor, ed., *Law and Interpretation* 329–56 (1995); Jeremy Waldron, "The Dignity of Legislation," 54 MD L. REV. 633 (1995).

130. Easterbrook has written of avoiding the "intentionalist fallacy." *See* Easterbrook, *supra* note 66, at 535 n. 3. *See also id.* at 547: "Because legislatures comprise many members, they do not have 'intents' or 'designs' hidden yet discoverable. Each member may or may not have a design. The body as a whole, however, has only outcomes."

131. *See, e.g.*, Max Radin, *supra* note 108.

tions. However, his analysis does not establish conclusions as absolute as those he reaches.

Waldron emphasizes that modern democratic legislatures are composed of many members (typically hundreds), that legislators represent diverse interests and perspectives, and that one cannot expect legislative debates to be the kinds of conversations that take place between people who know each other well and share a common understanding about life. In these conditions of legislation, formal rules are needed to govern debate and voting; and these rules focus attention on specific propositions to be considered, cast in the language of bills to be amended or not, to be adopted or rejected. The diverse outlooks of the legislators themselves—and the focus on text of the formal rules—should lead interpreters to concentrate on the text.[132]

Waldron further suggests that, given the way in which we should view modern legislatures, it becomes illogical for judges to attend to mental-state intentions. He writes, "We must ask, then, whether there is anything true in general about the way in which statutes are produced that makes appeal to legislators' intentions a proper strategy of interpretation. How we answer that question will depend on what we take to be the most helpful general model of the legislative process, so far as themes of authority are concerned."[133] Interestingly, Waldron acknowledges that, occasionally, circumstances

132. *See* "Dignity of Legislation," *supra* note 129, at 657–59.

133. *See* "Legislators' Intentions," *supra* note 129, at 331–32.

could make reliance on the intentions of a single legislator appropriate—one legislator introduces a bill, and others adopt it as a matter of comity towards him[134]—but Waldron draws no broader implications from that acknowledgment.

Waldron argues that one could have unintentional legislation; legislators might register preferences or opinions about desirable standards, and a machine might accommodate these into final provisions that would not directly reflect anyone's individual intentions. If the machine is a more extreme possibility of unintentional legislation than any actual legislative process, nevertheless it points toward the way in which actual laws may diverge from the actual intentions of particular legislators. Waldron argues that the results of the inputs of many legislators may lead to outcomes preferable to those that any particular legislators want.[135] People, thus, may have good reason to accord the outcome of a legislative process authority that they would not concede to any set of intentions of any group of legislators. Waldron concludes that we should abandon all talk of legislative intention; "[t]here is simply no fact of the matter concerning a legislature's

134. *Id.* at 331.

135. *Id.* at 342–51. He examines this subject from the perspective of utilitarianism, from the standpoint of a theorem, developed by Condorcet (a French Enlightenment philosopher and mathematician), that the probability of desirable results may increase as the size of a legislative group increases, and from an Aristotelian assumption that diverse inputs increase the likelihood of desirable results (even when individuals may not grasp the wisdom of the inputs).

intentions apart from the formal specification of the act it has performed."[136]

Waldron is right that models of democratic legislatures can be very helpful, and that jurisprudential scholars have neglected the subject; but in three respects he moves too quickly from his general model to practical conclusions. First, he seems to assume that conclusions will necessarily be good for all democratic legislatures. That might be the result of a full analysis of similarities and differences, but it should not be a starting premise. Second, he assumes that courts in any system should have a uniform approach to intentions, independent of the kind of legislation and the actual process that has produced statutory provisions. An alternative possibility is that courts should be sensitive to various nuances in subject matter and legislative process. Perhaps this contextual approach is too complicated for judges and critics, but we cannot dismiss it out of hand. Third, Waldron assumes that his model captures the essence of all legislative behavior or that it captures enough of it so that the model should inform the approach of judicial interpreters. However, whether a critic supposes that judges should make nuanced assessments of the ways that particular pieces of legislation are enacted or considers the one right "model" to inform all statutory interpretation in a particular system, he needs to gauge how well the model fits the ordinary reality. If, in practice, an intentions approach would make sense for many occasions, its uncomfortable fit with

136. *Id.* at 353.

a chosen ideal model and with *some* actual exercises of legislative power is not a sufficient ground to reject the approach altogether.

I shall develop two American examples, but first I make a comment about legislatures with cabinet governments in which a majority party controls both houses (or controls the house with the real power—as when a party controls the House of Commons in Great Britain). Party members in the legislature in Great Britain have a powerful say in choosing who will be the party's prime minister, who then appoints other members of the cabinet;[137] but in modern times, members of the majority party almost invariably *vote* for bills the cabinet recommends (except those the cabinet advertises as free votes). The language of bills, perhaps partly settled after committee consideration, usually does not change greatly in response to broader legislative debates, although the government is somewhat responsive to concerned members of its own party and even to complaints from members of the opposition. When legislation is in a particular subject area, professional staff and the cabinet, and committee members with authority in that area, are largely responsible for a bill's details. Thus, a rather tight circle of civil servants and like-minded legislators decides most of the details of statutes, and, according to strict party loyalty, proposed bills are virtually certain of approval (especially if the party in

137. The "say" is somewhat greater in the Conservative Party than in the Labour Party. E. C. S. Wade & A. W. Bradley, *Constitutional and Administrative Law* 254 (A. W. Bradley & K. D. Ewing, 11th ed. 1993).

power has a handy majority.)[138] Individual legislators rarely base their votes on a judgment about
whether they approve of the main objectives of a
particular bill.

This account does not correspond exactly with the
conditions under which Waldron thinks reference to
legislative intentions would be appropriate—the bill
introduced by a single legislator, which others adopt
as a matter of comity—but the account comes closer
to those conditions than it does to the engine of
unintentional legislation or to the model of provisions arrived at after contributions from highly
diverse sources, which play such prominent roles in
Waldron's analysis.

Justice Breyer provides an American example involving the power of federal bankruptcy courts to
adjudicate "core proceedings" without the consent
of the parties.[139] The legislative history indicates
that those who drafted and thought about the
phrase intended it to allow adjudication of all claims
that were within the constitutional power of federal
bankruptcy courts. "Core proceedings" is not a
phrase that emerged from the give and take of
legislative debate, a phrase that might perhaps be

138. *See* Atiyah and Summers, *supra* note 11, at 299–306,
315–23. Professor Waldron has pointed out to me that conditions
of legislation can vary significantly. On occasion, a party with a
plurality has had to rely on some fringe party to make up a
majority. For some especially important legislation, the party in
power has deemed it important to have support from members of
the other major party, and thus cannot rely entirely on loyal
votes of its own party members.

139. Breyer, *supra* note 58, at 854–56.

"wiser" than the intentions of any individual legislator. The phrase was apparently picked to accomplish a fairly technical objective, and its exact scope was not a matter of concern for the vast majority of legislators. This example, if I am correct about its force, also comes fairly close to Waldron's conditions for appropriate use of intentions.

My second American example is rather different. During the Great Depression most states, wishing to avoid the cutthroat competition of "price wars," had adopted "fair trade" legislation, allowing manufacturers to fix retail prices of their products with retailers who sold them. After an initial beginning in California, in which the prices fixed were set only for those retailers who agreed, all states with such laws, California among them, included non-signer clauses. These provided that, under state law, non-signing retailers could not charge less than the signing retailers had agreed to charge. Thus a manufacturer's agreement with one or two retailers could bind hundreds of non-signing retailers. The states' fair-trade laws were doubly at odds with basic federal antitrust laws, under which manufacturers and retailers could not agree on retail prices, and states could not require retailers to fix prices (as the non-signer clauses provided).

Congress adopted the Miller–Tydings Act to create an antitrust exception to allow states' fair-trade laws. The crucial provision said, "nothing ... shall render illegal, contracts or agreements prescribing minimum prices for the resale" of certain commodities when those contracts or agreements are made lawful for intrastate transactions.[140] A liquor manufacturer sued a *non-signing* retailer, and the U.S. Supreme Court had to decide whether the federal provision validated Louisiana's non-signer clause. The textual language is ambiguous but lends itself to the construction that it approves only the actual agreements to fix prices, not the application to non-signers.[141] Both the development of state laws, reflecting uniform judgments that fair-trade laws were ineffective without non-signer clauses, and the legislative history of the Miller–Tydings Act indicated strongly that most legislators (or at least most who had thought about the issue) wanted to "validate" the non-signer clauses, and believed that the statutory language did so.[142] Here the interpretive issue was an either-or choice, on which the effectiveness of a significant piece of legislation turned. It is conceivable that the contributions of diverse

140. Schwegmann Bros. v. Calvert Distillers Corp., 341 U.S. 384 (1951). The statute is 50 Stat. 693, 15 U.S.C. § 1.

141. The majority of the Court decided that the act was limited in this way.

142. See the dissenting opinion of Frankfurter, J., 341 U.S., at 399–411. This case does have a wrinkle that may matter. Possibly those in Congress wanted to coerce the non-signers but wished to use language that would not explicitly say so. It is a serious question, whether intentional efforts to conceal or obscure effects of laws should be rewarded. Given notions of publicity in legislation, judges definitely should not pay attention to completely secret purposes. The difficult issue here is whether they should pay attention to a purpose that is consistent with one reading of the language and with legislative history, but which legislators may have chosen not to emphasize by their choice of statutory language.

sources led to the particular textual formulation; but when the choice is either-or in this way—and most legislators have a view that the language is to be read one way rather than the other—Waldron's model does not seem a good reason to relegate intentions to irrelevance.[143]

IV. Conclusion

Judicial references to legislative intentions are often ambiguous about whether mental-state intentions or some objective notion of intent are meant. Whether judges should consider the mental states of participants in the legislative process is debatable. Certain "knock down" arguments against such consideration based on the nature of modern legislation and on restrictions on methods of enacting statutes are not convincing. The possible relevance of intentions might depend partly on how legislation is adopted, the relative expertness of legislators, and whether those at whom a statute is directed stand in a cooperative relationship with the legislature.

If inquiry into mental-state intentions is different from other techniques of interpretation, legal interpretation certainly should not depend *entirely* on

143. However, I should note both that Waldron's overall view would allow these sources to affect interpretation, though not through the vehicle of intentions, and that the dissent's position that the federal act validated non-signer clauses could be supported on the basis of purpose and coherence with other law in a manner that did not refer to mental states of legislators.

inferences about intentions. For many statutes, however, knowable mental-state intentions should be relevant for interpretation, *unless* discovering them is too cumbersome, or relying on them will cause more harm than benefit in the interactions between legislatures and courts.

CHAPTER IX

WHICH MENTAL STATES SHOULD COUNT?

In this and the following chapter, I discuss which mental states of which persons might count. Seven points can help clarify the ensuing discussion. First, if we fail to develop any coherent sense of the mental states that are relevant, that would be a powerful reason for rejecting a mental-states approach. Second, these questions about mental states are relevant not only for those who think that intentions are the central key to interpretation; a person who assigns such mental states any weight at all needs to resolve these questions in some manner. Third, in contrast to the typical assumption that, for all laws, a convincing theory would rely upon a single mental state, on analysis, more than one mental state may be relevant, and the best approach may vary for different laws. Fourth, although one may ask what constitutes a relevant "intention," the critical question is not which mental states of legislators amount to intentions (in the ordinary sense of intentions), but which mental states should count for judicial interpretation. Fifth, the classes of persons whose mental states count may depend on the type of legislation and legislative body. Sixth, even if mental states should sometimes

117

be relevant, Waldron may be right that mental states should not count in respect to some statutory provisions. Seventh, a plausible approach must reach adjustment between that which ideally is to count and that which judges can discover. If the mental states that ideally should count, are wholly undiscoverable, one has to propose that judges look for other mental states, introduce objective elements into an inquiry about mental states, or acknowledge ..., to propose that judges look for other mental states introduced "objective" elements into an inquiry about mental states, or acknowledge that mental-state intentions should not be a criterion of interpretation. In this and the next chapter, I assume that mental states are completely knowable; in Chapter Eleven I address crucial issues about discoverability.

I. Which Mental States?

This chapter addresses the subject of Question 7: Which mental states should count?[144] Matters would be simplest if statutes were adopted unanimously by legislators, all of whom have carefully considered and discussed the text. In these conditions, remote indeed from typical modern legislation, the mental states of all legislators should count and (at least if participation were roughly equal) should count equally. We can imagine at least three mental states that might be relevant: (1) hopes, (2) expectations, and (3) a sense of proper interpretation.[145]

144. "If mental-state intentions count, which mental states, actual or hypothetical, matter?"

145. Ronald Dworkin has suggested a fourth possible "mental state." *See* Ronald Dworkin, *supra* note 6, at 327–33 (1986).

At first glance, we might think that the hopes of legislators would be most significant.[146] If legislators chose statutory language without compromise, *and* administrators and judges were to apply a statute on behalf of a public that had no perceived interests in opposition to aims of the legislators, hopes would be a good guide for interpretation. Those applying the law could seek to carry out the will of the legislators, thus fulfilling their aspirations.

We can see quickly why hopes should not be an exclusive guide if, as is usually the case, statutory terms result from compromise, or important addressees have interests or convictions opposed to those of the legislators, or both. The language of the Selective Service Act of 1940 offers an apt illustration. The law created an exemption for conscientious objectors whose opposition to participation in war was based on "religious training and belief," defined, after 1948, to include belief in a "Supreme

This is his third alternative, since he does not consider views about proper interpretation. He talks about a legislator's overall convictions and how a statute fits with them. This "convictions approach" is a possible guide to interpretation, but it has little to do with actual mental states at the time legislation is adopted. Since a legislator may agree to language that he does not think accords with his overall convictions, these convictions are a poor guide to his mental-state intentions about much particular language. Moreover, convictions change; a legislator's past convictions need not reflect his mental-state intentions when he votes for a new law. Dworkin, himself, does not defend a "convictions" approach. It is a stalking horse for his own favored method of interpretation.

146. Paul Brest, *supra* note 36, at 209–11 (1980). Problems with relying on hopes, or expectations, are examined forcefully in Dworkin, *Law's Empire*, *supra* note 6, at 321–24.

Being." In 1965 the U.S. Supreme Court interpreted this language not to require belief in a "Supreme Being,"[147] and, five years later, it said the provision does not require religious belief in any ordinary sense.[148] Omitting other substantial arguments for these results,[149] I here develop various (unrealistic) hypothetical assumptions to ask whether the statute, according to mental-state-intention analysis, exempted atheists who were conscientious objectors.

Let us suppose, first, that virtually all members of Congress personally wished exemptions for atheists but feared that any explicit provision to that effect would anger draft boards and constituents. Unwilling to take the heat for exempting atheists, they voted for language that apparently limited the exemption to *theists*. Each legislator hoped that judges would interpret the statute to cover atheists. Each would then have the outcome he or she wished, but judges would bear the responsibility for it. If legislators believed that judges would not interpret the statute to exempt atheists and, further, thought that such an extension would be an unjustifiable stretch of judicial power, the legislators could hardly be said to have intended to exempt atheists by this language. Their hopes should have no relevance at all, or should have much less

147. United States v. Seeger, 380 U.S. 163 (1965).

148. Welsh v. United States, 398 U.S. 333 (1970). Strictly, only a plurality of four reached this conclusion in *Welsh*. Justice Harlan concurred on constitutional grounds.

149. The strongest arguments draw on constitutional values of free exercise and nonestablishment.

relevance than what they imagined they were creating as law.

Now suppose, instead, that the language was a compromise between those who wanted no exemption for conscientious objectors at all, and those who wanted to exempt atheists as well as theists. They settled on exempting the least controversial category, theistic conscientious objectors to all wars. All legislators understood the textual language to have this limited effect, but it turns out that those who wanted atheists as well as theists to be exempted were in a slight majority. They compromised about the language because they were unsure whether they had a majority and because they regarded near unanimity as important. Again, these legislators' hope that judges would extend the statute to atheists hardly makes this their crucial mental-state intention in adopting language they conceived as definitely not going that far.

Do legislators' expectations matter more than their hopes? A legislator may have limited confidence in the present courts; he may worry that judges will probably misinterpret certain language. Such beliefs about likely judicial errors should not ordinarily count for what a statute means; a legislator does not intend language to be construed mistakenly, even though he thinks incompetent judges are likely to do so.[150] We can see from the conscientious-objector statute that even hopes and expectations together need not constitute a rele-

150. I qualify this conclusion below in a very important respect.

vant intention. A member of Congress may have hoped atheists would be exempted, and may have predicted that a very liberal U.S. Supreme Court would probably do so, but if he thought the language could not reasonably be understood in that way, he did not intend that result in a way that should count for a court.

A more appealing standard than either hopes or expectations is how legislators believe language should be interpreted. If a legislator believes that judges *should* understand language in a certain way, is it not his or her intention that it be so understood? There are three difficulties here, but each can be met.

One is the question of interpretation by whom. It is conceivable that a legislator might think that initial addressees, say private persons or draft boards, should understand language in one way but that courts should understand it in another. I shall pass over this complexity, assuming that legislators suppose that the right interpretation will be the same for everyone.

The second problem is more troublesome. Statutory interpretation is a complicated business, at which judges are more expert than legislators. Should judges be guided by the cruder notions of legislators about how judges should do their jobs? This approach would seem misguided, if not destructively circular. Fortunately, there are ways out of this dilemma. The simplest way out is to say that legislators' notions of proper interpretation determine their intentions, but mental-state intentions are only one ingredient, not the final criterion of proper judicial interpretation. Thus, judges, though giving some weight to intentions, need not actually follow the less expert views of legislators about interpretation. Another possibility is for judges to distinguish ordinary understanding of language from other relevant aspects of interpretation. The relevant mental-state intentions of legislators might concern the way primary addressees and judges should understand language, putting aside those complexities of interpretation at which judges are most expert.[151] According to this possibility, judges could avoid giving any weight at all to views of legislators about subjects at which judges are more expert.[152]

151. It might be answered that this distinction is artificial, that legislators do not distinguish the way the language should be understood, putting aside interpretive complexities, and the way it should be understood, period. It is probably true that legislators do not think in terms of this distinction, but that need not undermine its relevance. One may conceive of a crucial mental-state intention that is artificial or hypothetical: what legislators would think about ordinary (or expert) understanding of the language. Or, one may acknowledge that a legislator's mental-state intention is usually about interpretation overall, but claim that the intention should not guide judges when it reaches complexities of interpretation at which judges are especially expert.

152. People may, of course, debate just which are the aspects of interpretation at which judges are more expert. An approach that lies between the two mentioned in the text would be for judges to give *some* weight to the legislators' full view of proper interpretation but to discount to a degree for components at which judges are more expert. I explore these nuances in greater

The third problem about a legislator's understanding of how language should be interpreted involves a tension between existing interpretive practice and the legislator's ideal for that practice. This problem reintroduces the relevance of expectations when a legislator has a certain attitude about what the courts are doing.

Suppose a legislator has developed a definite view about the way judges should understand certain kinds of statutory language. As a legislator, however, he takes dominant interpretive practice as the context for his legislative activities.[153] Like many other actors in the political system, he accepts, as a kind of given, decisions made by others in their spheres of special competence.[154] He realizes that few judges employ his favored perspective about interpretation. He agrees to compromise language that he wants in order to produce a certain result, and he knows judges will interpret that language in order to reach the desired outcome. He actually believes that judges *should* require other, more explicit, language to reach that result. He does not regard a fight for the more explicit language as

depth in "Are Mental States Relevant for Statutory and Constitutional Interpretation?," an article to be published.

153. One might compare his attitude to that of a district court judge who resolves cases in light of U.S. Supreme Court precedents and practices of interpretation with which she disagrees.

154. Joseph Raz has written of legislators who intend to enact statutes that will be interpreted according to accepted conventions for interpretation. Raz, "Intention in Interpretation," in *The Autonomy of Law* 249, 268–69 (Robert George, ed., 1996).

worthwhile, since he views it as practically unneces-
sary. We may say that the legislator who accepts
dominant judicial practice as part of the legislative
environment intends the statutory language to
achieve the result he wants and expects, even
though he thinks that ideally the language should
be interpreted otherwise.[155] The legislator's crucial
state of mind is something more complicated than a
simple hope, expectation, or belief about proper
interpretation.

If we focus on actual mental states, the single
state of mind that should be most relevant is how a
legislator believes language should be understood,
under interpretive practices that he accepts as giv-
en. But it does not follow that every other state of
mind should be treated as wholly irrelevant. If the
proper interpretation seems otherwise very close, a
legislator's hopes should matter to some degree. If
language could easily be read in one of two ways,
and judges could somehow know that legislators
divided evenly about how it should be interpreted,
the judges should be influenced to a degree by the
knowledge that virtually all legislators *wanted* the
language to be construed in one of those ways, in
order to achieve desirable consequences. The critical
issue for judges, we must remember, is not exactly
which mental states constitute intentions but which
mental states of those who legislate should influence those responsible for interpretation.

155. This represents the qualification to the proposition in
text from which *supra* note 150 is dropped.

II. Levels of Intention

As I have mentioned, legislators may have mental-state intentions that concern both the specific details of a provision and the further aims that lie behind it and related provisions. In accordance with what I have said about intentions more generally, we need to understand a legislator's view about purposes as grounded in his sense of what the law's underlying objectives should be taken to be, not as a simple reflection of his personal hopes or his estimates of what courts will do. A racist with a large minority constituency may accept racial equality as an underlying purpose of a law, although he actually hopes that purpose will be frustrated and believes a conservative judiciary may do so.

An interpreter may conclude that fulfilling their specific intentions about a provision would frustrate the legislators' main purposes. How should the interpreter then be guided by mental-state intentions? Two different strategies might be used to resolve this sort of difficulty.

One strategy carries further a mental-state approach; it calls on judges to be as faithful as possible to the intentions of the legislators. Suppose, for example, the legislators have a clear purpose and a clear, specific intention; they embrace the latter to promote the former because of a mistaken factual judgment. Most legislators conceived Title VII of the Civil Rights Act of 1964 as directed at eliminating conscious racial discrimination against blacks. Many legislators, if not most, supposed that the act would forbid voluntary racial categorization *in favor* of blacks.[156] What they (arguably) failed to realize was that, unless companies could engage in voluntary affirmative action of that kind, they would have little incentive to remedy past racial discrimination against blacks until previous violations were formally established. Given limited enforcement resources, the correction of past violations would be considerably greater if voluntary affirmative action were allowed than if it were forbidden. On this account,[157] implementing the legislators' specific intent about voluntary affirmative action would seriously undermine enforcement against the kind of racial discrimination the legislators mainly aimed to stop. Suppose U.S. Supreme Court justices recognized this conflict and also realized that few legislators had perceived it. If the justices attempted to carry out the intentions of the legislators insofar as they could, they would have had to determine which

156. United Steelworkers of America v. Weber, 443 U.S. 193 (1979), already discussed in *supra* Chapter Six.

157. Nothing about preferences for minorities is uncontroversial, but I can claim for my account here that it is close to the position taken in a concurring opinion of Justice Blackmun, in Weber, 443 U.S. at 211, 214–15, and that I believe it to be sound. My point does not depend on the account's soundness, however, since I offer it as an illustration of a more general possibility. As William Eskridge has shown (*Dynamic Statutory Interpretation*, *supra* note 84, at 25), Supreme Court and executive branch decisions after Title VII was adopted exacerbated the difficulty that employers would have faced if voluntary affirmative action had been held impermissible. *See also* Frickey, *supra* note 84, at 246–47. This point is developed in Chapter Seventeen.

of their intentions were dominant. The justices might think legislators had an opinion about whether specific intent or purpose should win out in such circumstances. If so, they would follow that opinion. If not, the Justices might be reduced to deciding what legislators probably would have taken as most important if they had become aware of this conflict[158] or (more generally) conflicts of this sort.

When a conflict of specific intent and purpose arises mainly from a normative shift in view, rather than new factual understanding, a court similarly could assess dominant intentions. Suppose that, when the Civil Rights Act was adopted, most legislators regarded explicit racial categorization as morally unacceptable, even if used to eliminate unfair working conditions over time. Further reflection has led most people to believe that such categorizations that favor members of previously oppressed groups are acceptable short-term expedients.[159] Drawing from widely held opinion, the justices have a different perception of the moral acceptability of affirmative action than did most of the enacting legislators. If the justices are to be guided by the

158. If they had become aware of the conflict before Title VII was enacted, legislators probably would have changed the language. It is possible, however, that legislators would be aware of such a conflict, but consider the issue so controversial that an attempt to resolve the conflict by a change in language might have unacceptable political costs, or even undermine the chances of adoption.

159. I am illustrating the basic possibility, *not* trying to capture actual attitudes about affirmative action, which have been strongly held and intensely divided, with swings in dominant opinion since 1964.

legislators' dominant intentions, they will try to figure out whether the legislators wished judges mainly to implement the legislators' specific evaluations or their broader purpose to fight employment discrimination in morally acceptable ways.

Andrei Marmor has suggested that, since specific applications are merely a means to pursue further intentions, "application intentions ought to be taken into account—from the legislator's own point of view—only if, and to the extent that, their realization is likely to enhance his further intentions."[160] On the simplistic assumptions that there is one legislator, that the conflict between specific and further intentions is undisputed, and that the rejection of the specific intention does not run up against any different purpose the legislator attaches to the statute, Marmor's conclusion is right. It becomes vulnerable once these unrealistic assumptions are dropped.

The interpreter may believe that specific and further intentions conflict; but that may be arguable. Should an interpreter abandon a means that legislators favored, on the basis of a probabilistic judgment that it is ill chosen? That is doubtful.

Rarely do purposes stand alone. Many legislators who aimed to correct past discrimination against blacks may also have believed that any racial categorization is inherently wrong.[161] An interpreter

160. Marmor, *supra* note 119, at 171.

161. Eliminating all racial categorization in employment might be regarded as a second further legislative intention or as

might doubt that legislators would accept voluntary racial categorization even if they recognized that doing so would further Title VII's main objective to a much greater degree than they had realized when they adopted the law. Relatedly, people who are brought to see a conflict between means and ends may find out they are more attached to the means— and less attached to the ends—than they previously grasped. The complex constellations of purposes and the untidiness of the way means may relate to ends should give judges pause in affording preeminence to purpose.

Finally, legislatures have many people. If the provision about means is clear, we know that that was actually adopted; views about underlying purposes and background values may have varied more considerably. Individual legislators who understand all of this might prefer that judges not undertake debatable conjectures about purpose. For all these reasons, an interpreter who identifies a conflict of specific intentions and purposes or further intentions cannot assume without more that legislators want their purposes to rule their specific intentions.

A different approach to conflicts of specific intention and purpose does not rely on legislators' views about how such conflicts should be resolved, but asks what emphasis best fits the interpretive process. Judges might decide that one kind of intention or the other is most helpful to follow in light of the comparative competence and authority of legisla-

a background value against which any means for increasing employment for blacks should be measured.

tures and courts. The appropriate emphasis might vary depending on the particular legal problem, the statute's language, and its age. Some reasons for preferring specific intentions or broader purposes relate to methods of discovery, discussed below; but even if judges could identify mental states with confidence, they would face competing reasons. They might prefer broader purposes because these last better through time than do narrowly conceived specific results, or they might prefer specific results because legislators have concentrated more carefully on those.

If judges decide, based on dominant legislative intentions or respective competence, that one level of intentions has priority, room should remain for consideration of the other. For example, if judges look mainly to specific intentions, but the specific circumstances were conceived by few or no legislators, judges should look to underlying purposes for a resolution. If judges look mainly to broader purposes, but these are indecisive, they should attend to specific intentions.

In general, assuming that the relevant mental states are adequately discoverable, judges should give weight to intentions both about specific resolutions and purposes. In determining comparative weight, judges should take actual dominant intentions of legislators into account when they are able to identify these; but they should also consider what emphasis will best reflect the comparative competence of courts and legislatures and contribute to a healthy interpretive process.

III. Hypothetical Intentions and Reconstructive Interpretation

A. *Hypothetical Intentions*

As to many specific matters that arise in litigation, few legislators will have had definite intentions. The problem is greatest for old statutes, now being applied to circumstances the legislators who adopted them did not foresee. A judge who focuses on mental states might ask how legislators would have resolved a matter if they had thought about it. What *would* legislators have concluded about some problem of interpretation they did not consider? Such hypothetical intentions raise concerns beyond those that accompany reliance on actual intentions. These concerns might conceivably lead someone to say that judges should assess *actual* mental states of legislators but not *hypothetical* ones; but an approach that gives weight to actual states presses in various ways to include hypothetical states.

One concern about hypothetical intentions is that they must be partly constructive. Ask yourself what you would have thought ten years ago about a problem you did not consider then. Even if you could remember every thought you have ever had, you could not be sure what you would have thought about some problems you never considered. Your present perspectives would be bound to influence your judgment.[162] This difficulty of discernment in-

162. You could, of course, try to "put yourself in the entire frame of mind that you had in years past"; but typically this will

creases greatly when one person assesses what another person *would have thought*, given much less information about the actual past thoughts of that other person. The temptation is great to suppose that the other person would have embraced what one now thinks is a good resolution. Still, the practical problems of discernment are not limited to hypothetical states of mind. One person often has difficulty estimating what another actually believes, unless the second person has expressed those beliefs clearly.

A second possible problem with hypothetical intentions involves various paradoxes about voting. Suppose the claim is put that any legislator's crucial hypothetical intention is determined by whether the legislator would have voted for language that would have resolved a disputed case, one way or the other. For various reasons, one may not be able to answer that question in a way that bears on what a court should decide about intent.

Theorists of social choice have discovered features about voting in legislative bodies that make it sometimes impossible to answer how a person would have voted on a particular issue.[163] Suppose the

be more difficult than recalling specific thoughts, feelings, and judgments.

163. *See* Dworkin, *supra* note 6, at 326–27. *See also* Kenneth Arrow, *Social Choice and Individual Values* (2nd ed. 1963); William H. Riker and Barry R. Weingast, "Constitutional Regulation of Legislative Choice: The Political Consequences of Judicial Deference to Legislators," 74 VA L. REV. 373 (1988); Frickey, *supra* note 84, at 252–53; Eskridge, *supra* note 84, at 16, 36–37,

question is whether a legislator would have voted for *b*, *b* being one possible interpretation of unclear language. He prefers *a* to *b*, and *b* to *c*. He would have voted for *b* if it had been paired against *c*, *a* already having been defeated. But he would have voted against *b* if it had been paired against *a*, *c* already having been defeated. This means his vote on *b* would have depended on the order in which alternatives were considered; whether he would have favored *b* would have depended on when *b* was put to a vote.

We cannot assume any natural order of voting here, with the two most appealing alternatives considered last. One reason why there may be no natural order of voting is because of the phenomenon of *cycling*. For example, given different orders of preferences among different legislators, it may be that *a* would win against *b*, *b* against *c*, and *c* against *a*. Each option may gain a majority against one alternative and fail to gain a majority against another. In large legislative bodies, the instability of outcomes that this cycling could cause is substantially mitigated by the power of committee chairs and others to control the agenda, and by the difficulty of relegislating. But it is highly doubtful that our legislator's hypothetical intention about unclear language should be determined in a particular way because the committee chair would be able to assure that *b* was matched against *c* rather than *a*.

222–24. *See generally* Daniel Farber and Philip Frickey, *Law and Public Choice: A Critical Introduction* (1991).

Another complicating factor is strategic voting. Legislators sometimes vote against discrete alternatives that they favor because they want to load a bill they do not like with enough controversial features so that it will be defeated.[164] Suppose a particular legislator would have voted for *b* if the issue had been clearly put at the stage it would have arisen, because he hoped that explicit inclusion of *b* would make the bill too controversial to pass. This strategic evaluation should not determine the legislator's intention about a law already passed, whose language is unclear as to whether it prescribes *b*.

Finally, there may be occasions when a legislator believes that language will accomplish an objective he wants and expects but would not be willing to support if it were set out in unmistakably clear language.[165] He may worry that clear endorsement of that objective would offend too many constituents. What courts should do when legislators purposefully disguise their objectives is a subject to which I shall return; here I note only that this possibility further compromises the idea of basing

164. See Riker and Weingast, *supra* note 163, at 389–91, on strategic voting about aid to education. The initial inclusion in Title VIII of coverage of gender discrimination was proposed by a representative who hoped to defeat the entire measure. *See* William Eskridge and Philip Frickey, *Cases and Materials on Legislation: Statutes and the Creation of Public Policy* 15–16 (1988).

165. *See* Jonathan Macey, "Promoting Public–Regarding Legislation Through Statutory Interpretation: An Interest–Group Model," 86 COLUM L. REV. 223, 232 (1986).

hypothetical intentions on imaginary votes, in order to resolve a contested legal issue.

Fortunately, we can largely (though not entirely) avoid these worries that either (1) one may not be able to determine how a legislator would have voted on the issue the court faces or (2) the legislator's vote would not fairly reflect his intention about the statute as it was actually adopted. I have suggested that the critical question about "specific intent" concerns the way a legislator, addressing the question at the moment of passage, thought the statute's language should be understood with respect to the problem the court faces. The parallel hypothetical question is about how a legislator would have thought the language for which he *did* vote should reasonably be understood with respect to that problem. Would he have believed that the language prescribes *b* or not? If we conceive of the hypothetical inquiry as an either-or question of whether the statutory language requires a particular result, this formulation of hypothetical intention is not subject to the drawbacks of uncertain alternatives, cycling, agenda control, or strategic voting that can arise from hypothetical questions about preferences.[166]

166. Matters may not be so simple, however, if the crucial decision in a case is among three or more possible interpretations or if there are vital disagreements about the meaning of statutory language and about the application of a particular meaning to the facts of the case. Louis Kornhauser and Lawrence Sager discuss a somewhat similar problem with the votes of members of a court. "The One and the Many: Adjudication in Collegial Courts," 81 CALIF L. REV. 1 (1993). But, it should be noted, as the Kornhauser and Sager article illustrates, that these difficulties can arise from actual states of mind as much as from hypotheti-

Whatever the difficulties of hypothetical intentions, most interpretive strategies that give significant weight to actual understandings incline toward giving weight to hypothetical understandings as well. This is true for three, possibly four, reasons.

The first reason concerns discovery. A court that is interested in the attitudes of most legislators will have a difficult (perhaps impossible) task in figuring out just what subjects crossed the minds of legislators. Further, a court will often doubt whether enough legislators had actual specific understandings about a subject. If judges can give weight to hypothetical intentions, the need to settle exactly which actual intentions existed is lessened. The strength of this reason for using hypothetical intentions diminishes somewhat if one emphasizes purpose to the exclusion of specific intentions. At least for major legislation, virtually all legislators will have some sense of a law's broad purposes. Indeed, one may think of much interpretation as involving judicial use of actual purposes to draw out hypothetical judgments about narrower, more specific issues.

A second reason for judges giving weight to hypothetical intentions concerns similar treatment of closely related factual circumstances. Suppose legislators have thought about a number of situations and have a clear view that each should be resolved

cal ones. *See also* Frank Easterbrook, "Ways of Criticizing the Court," 95 HARV. L. REV. 802, 816 (1982); Richard Fallon, Jr., "Foreword: Implementing the Constitution," 111 HARV L. REV. 54, 109, n. 316 (1997).

in a particular way under the statutory language. The actual case involves a slightly different factual circumstance that the legislators definitely did not consider, and that the terms of the statutory language do not clearly embrace or exclude. If judges are going to deal with all of the problems legislators have considered, in the way the legislators conceived, the judges should treat this similar case as covered by the statutory language. Here, judges could easily reach a conclusion about the legislators' hypothetical intentions, and they should follow it.

An opponent of reliance on hypothetical intentions could concede this practical conclusion but propose an alternative avenue to reach it. He could say that results of cases should be consonant with actual mental-state intentions. Judges should decide cases that were unforeseen by legislators, in order to correspond best with the results the legislators consciously intended. Judges might treat the results covered by actual intentions as like precedents to guide decision in novel, unforeseen situations. (Insofar as judges rely on actual purposes to resolve problems about specific applications that were not conceived, the strategy could similarly be conceptualized in a way that does not depend on hypothetical judgments.) Although the exercise of making judicial decisions correspond with actual intentions is conceptually different from judicial inquiry about hypothetical intentions, the approaches are closely similar in practice. Judges, reasoning by analogy, are guided by actual intentions to determine hypothetical intentions or to determine an appropriate fit of results.

Changing conditions constitute a third reason to consider hypothetical intentions. As circumstances become less and less like those that any legislators had in mind, it becomes harder and harder to suppose that they had an actual intent about the way unclear language should be construed with respect to the situation a court faces. If circumstances are unexpected enough, the answer to the disputed legal issue may be unfairly determined by the way a court puts the question about actual intent. In a series of well-known cases, courts considered the effect of the Nineteenth Amendment— which guaranteed women the right to vote—on state laws that made "persons" who were qualified to vote liable for jury service.[167] Some courts asked whether those who adopted the state law in the previous century intended their language to cover women. The answer was that those legislators were assuming only men would be jurors. But at least as appropriate a question about actual intent was whether the legislators intended the class of people eligible for jury service to change with changes in the class that was eligible to vote. The answer to that question would have been "yes"; the legislators assumed that the elimination of some barriers to voting, such as a property qualification, would alter the class eligible to sit on juries. Once one

167. *See, e.g.*, Commonwealth v. Welosky, 276 Mass. 398, 177 N.E. 656 (1931), discussed with other cases in Hart and Sacks, *supra* note 80, at 1172–85.

notes that the change in voter eligibility that the Nineteenth Amendment wrought was much vaster and more radical than the earlier legislators were likely to have had in mind, one realizes that actual intent may not resolve the case. But one might ask, "Had the legislators conceived of the mandatory inclusion of woman as part of the class of voters, would they have assumed that the class of eligible jurors would expand accordingly?" One, thus, could pose a hypothetical question that is fairly phrased to capture the issue in the case.[168] To be clear, I am not suggesting the case should be resolved on this basis; it is highly doubtful that a statute with general language about "persons" should be construed in accord with outdated attitudes of past male legislators toward the prospect of women serving on juries. I am only suggesting that, insofar as one focuses on actual intent, the tendency to move to hypothetical intent for older statutes is considerable.

A final possible reason to pay some attention to hypothetical intent concerns the respective weight to give to specific intentions and further intentions. If legislators have not considered future conflicts of that sort, and judges wish to identify dominant intentions, judges may need recourse to hypotheti-

168. Perhaps my inclusion of the word "mandatory" is debatable. More critically, it may be argued that one should consider legislators who have modern attitudes toward women. The more one alters such fundamental attitudes of the actual legislators, the less the question becomes a hypothetical one about *their* intentions.

cal intentions in order to decide which intentions were dominant.

B. Reconstructive Interpretation

Some strategies of interpretation give a central place to hypothetical intentions. In a Supreme Court opinion, Justice Cardozo cast the problem of meaning as "which choice is it the more likely that Congress would have made?"[169] At one stage, Judge Posner argued that the task of the judge is to engage in imaginative reconstruction. For situations in which the enactment is unclear, Posner suggested that the right question to frame is like that of a platoon commander who asks, "What would the company commander have wanted me to do if communication failed?"[170] Posner writes, "You can be creative in imagining how someone else would have acted knowing what you know as well as what he knows."[171] As I have mentioned, in a case involving the scale of punishments for sellers of LSD, Posner, in dissent, was willing to stretch the ordinary meaning of the directly applicable language to a substantial degree in order to arrive at a sentencing struc-

169. Burnet v. Guggenheim, 288 U.S. 280, 285 (1933). Felix Frankfurter, *supra* note 98, at 539, mentioned this formulation approvingly but cautioned that it "too often tempts inquiry into the subjective...."

170. Posner, *supra* note 125, at 190.

171. *Id.* at 200. See also Lawrence Lessig's proposal that, in changed circumstances, fidelity to a directive involves a kind of translation of its original application. "Fidelity in Translation," 71 Tex. L. Rev. 1165 (1993).

ture that was minimally rational in its comparative treatment of different offenders.[172]

What ties imaginative reconstruction so clearly to hypothetical intentions? Posner begins by seeking the main purpose(s) of a statute, based on the actual aims of those in the legislature.[173] From these purposes, he draws out the interpretation the legislators would have wanted for the case the judges must decide, even if that is at substantial variance with the specific language the statute uses. If the legislators had had a clear intent about a specific resolution, they would probably have chosen different language (unless they wanted to keep their intentions hidden). If the judges asked what they (the judges) would think would best carry out actual legislative purposes, they would not be framing the issue in terms of hypothetical intent. It is the emphasis on the way the legislators would have resolved an issue they did not face that makes hypothetical intention so central to imaginative reconstruction. The difficulties with this approach for

172. United States v. Marshall, 908 F. 2d. 1312, 1336 (7th Cir.1990) (en banc), *aff'd sub nom*. Chapman v. United States, 500 U.S. 453 (1991). In another case, West Va. Univ. Hosp. v. Casey, 499 U.S. 83, 100 (1991), Justice Scalia responded for a majority of the Court to Judge Posner's idea that "a court should 'complete ... the statute by reading it to bring about the end that the legislators would have specified had they thought about it more clearly.'" Scalia answered, "This . . profoundly mistakes our role." *See also* Chisom v. Roemer, 501 U.S. 380, 404–05 (1990) (Scalia, J., dissenting).

173. Posner has distinguished his view from that of Hart and Sacks, who suggest that judges should assume that legislators are reasonable and are acting reasonably in the public interest. Posner, *supra* note 125, at 192.

hidden purposes, compromises, and old statutes help explain why Posner himself has moved toward a position that assigns the judges more direct responsibility for achieving a desirable resolution of unclear language.[174]

IV. Conclusion

Our examination of which mental states of legislators should count, if any count, has revealed that neither hopes nor expectations are of overriding importance. The single state of mind that should be most relevant is the way legislators believe language should be understood, under interpretive practices they accept as given. Judges should, however, disregard or discount understandings based on aspects of interpretation at which they, the judges, are more expert.

Legislators may have understandings both about the specific coverage of provisions and about the underlying purposes of a statute. Judges may try to resolve perceived conflicts between these two, either in terms of the views of legislators or based on their own senses of desirable interpretive practice.

Although reliance on hypothetical understandings of legislators raises some special problems, any method that relies on actual understandings presses toward relying on hypothetical understandings as well. Some of the conclusions that public-choice

174. Posner, "Legislation and Its Interpretation—A Primer," 68 NEB. L. REV. 431, 445–46 (1989).

theory throws up against reliance on hypothetical intentions are largely avoided if the key understanding of legislators is the way statutory language should be understood. "Reconstructive interpretation" is an interpretive strategy that relies substantially on hypothetical intentions.

Chapter X

Whose Intentions Should Count, and in What Combinations?

This chapter faces the perplexing Question 8:[175] Whose intentions count, and in what combinations? On examination, there is *no single answer* either as to whose intentions should count or how much the intentions of some should count in comparison with the intentions of others.

I. Majorities, Minorities, and Combinations

One initially attractive possibility is that only the intentions of those who voted *for* a law count, and that enough of those legislators must believe (with whatever relevant mental state) that a law reaches certain behavior for that behavior to be covered by controlling mental-state intentions. Paul Brest has developed this notion of a majority of "intention votes" in a lucid way.[176] But this option presents an

175. "If mental states count, whose mental states matter, and what comparative weight do they have?"

176. Brest, *supra* note 36, at 209–13. However, I am not clear from Brest's discussion whether he thinks the intentions of a negative voter might count if the negative voter wanted the law to cover the doubtful situation and voted against the law only because of some unrelated provision of which he disapproved.

obvious difficulty. Suppose a vote is 50–49. One member of the majority—ill informed or upset—has extremely idiosyncratic views about coverage, and he does not think the law forbids behavior that all 98 other voters are sure is covered. Concluding that legislative intentions do not cover the behavior, because only 49 of 99 legislators voted in favor of covering it, is not plausible.[177]

A more general point indirectly highlighted by the 50–49 vote illustration is that when legislatures are genuine collective bodies, in which members work together to find appropriate language, the views of those who participate should count to some degree, even if they finally vote against a bill. This is obviously true if their negative votes do not concern the specific problem at issue; but it is also true when the very provision explains their vote against the bill. This point is clearest if we imagine a very small, intimate, council of legislators; such as three adult members a family. If only two finally accept a formulation that has been discussed at length, the views of the third about what the formu-

Ronald Dworkin has commented, "If the theory of legislative intent is to remain faithful to democratic principles, however, a minimum requirement must be met: a sufficient number of those who voted for a statute must have an understanding in common, so that that number alone could have passed the statute even if everyone else—all those who did not share that understanding—had voted against." "How to Read the Civil Rights Act," in Dworkin, *supra* note 84, at 322.

177. On the "vote to cover" theory, it would be conceivable that no behavior would be covered (if at least one of the fifty positive voters thought for some reason any particular behavior would not be covered).

lation covers should not be rendered irrelevant. Whenever legislators work together over language, with input by, and concessions to, members likely to vote against a bill in the final vote, the intentions of dissenters are relevant. The views of dissenters have less importance in systems where party loyalty assures a majority for whatever measures the government puts forward for a party vote. If negotiations with the opposition are minimal, the views of opposition members about what a law does should count for very little.

As these remarks suggest, one cannot reach a decisive answer about whose intentions count, and for how much, absent a sense of the actual legislative process. This process can differ significantly not only among political systems but also among laws adopted by the same legislature. Intentions of those in the majority should normally count the most; and a substantial majority of these should usually determine overall intentions (even if this majority falls short of an absolute majority of those voting).

This brings us to two related questions. What comparative weight should judges assign to the intentions of participants? Should judges take intentions into account even if they do not constitute majority intentions in any relevant sense?

Judges should assign more weight to the views of those who have considered a matter closely than to the views of fringe participants.[178] This approach is not antidemocratic. If one is to take the "temper"

178. *See* Dickerson, note 14, at 73.

of a group, one pays special attention to those who are most involved with the matter at hand. Typically, fringe participants will have no opinion whatsoever on the way some particular statutory language is to be understood. In that event, it is appropriate for an interpreter to consider the views of those who have considered the problem. Some aspects of this suggestion are by no means obvious, and they deserve exploration.

We need initially to recognize that the practical relevance of mental-state intentions about specific coverage turns largely on how we deal with the problem of participants who are ignorant or silent. Only rarely when a text is unclear in context will most voters have had a definite, ascertainable, opinion about the way it should be interpreted. If mental-state intentions count for interpretation only when some majority has shown that it shares an intention, there will be few instances when mental-state intentions will make a difference.

Once we grasp firmly why mental-state intentions may count, we should concede the relevance of intentions constituting less than a majority. Although people have trouble formulating the precise difference between statutory instructions themselves and the intentions underlying them, virtually everyone now agrees that there is a difference.[179] The statutory language is the subject of a formal

179. With informal individual instructions, it is arguable that a clear, known, intention about the instruction's meaning sometimes shades into the instruction. *See* Greenawalt, *supra* note 18, at 1004.

vote; it has an official status not quite like that of any intentions that are not reflected in the statute itself.[180] Yet, we have seen that strong reasons often support interpreting unclear instructions in accordance with the understanding of those who issued them. Now, imagine a rule is voted unanimously by a body of one hundred people. What the text seems to mean for the issue at hand is highly debatable. Eighty legislators have no opinion about the way it should be interpreted in context, but the remaining twenty all agree that it should be interpreted in a particular way. If the mental states of those issuing instructions can count, should an interpreter give *no weight* to the opinions of the twenty, even if the case is otherwise very close? So long as the twenty do not appear to be unrepresentative in an important way—for example favoring interests the other eighty do not—it makes sense for an interpreter to construe meaning to conform to their understanding. My claim here is meant to be modest. Because voting is formal and by majority, I do not claim that the intentions of a few should, by themselves, count heavily for interpretation, but only that these intentions should be given some weight in disputes that are otherwise difficult to resolve.

There are less stark ways to approach the problem of ignorant participants, ways that create a bridge from the few to the majority. These ways are very important, whether or not one agrees with my

180. Insofar as the intentions are put in a preamble, they have a formal status somewhat like that of operative language. Statutes that explicitly incorporate legislative history also give a formal status to evidences of intention.

claim that the intentions of less than a majority may have some relevance, in and of themselves. If I am wrong in that claim, the bridge to majority sentiments is necessary to give the intentions of the few *any* relevance whatsoever. But a bridge matters even if I am right. It matters because the intentions of the few will count for more if they can somehow be tied to the majority than if they stand alone.

The three possible bridges, not mutually exclusive, are hypothetical intentions, delegation, and convention. The argument about hypothetical intentions is straightforward. If eighty have not thought about a problem, and twenty have a certain opinion, the chances are good that most of the other eighty would come to the same conclusion if they addressed the issue. One method of ascribing hypothetical intentions to some is by reference to what others actually think.

Another possibility, suggested in various opinions, is "delegation."[181] The most straightforward idea of delegation is that less active legislators actually choose to delegate to more active and knowledgeable colleagues the formation of relevant mental states.[182] Such delegation may be especially likely

181. *See, e.g.,* Securities and Exch. Comm'n v. Robert Collier & Co., 76 F. 2d 939, 941 (2d Cir. 1935); Bank One Chicago, N.A. v. Midwest Bank & Trust Co., 516 U.S. 264, 277 (1996) (Stevens, J., concurring). Justice Scalia, *supra* note 4, at 35, suggests that any version of delegation is unconstitutional. If, unlike Scalia, one thinks reliance on intentions is otherwise appropriate, some delegation doctrine is a highly plausible aspect of intentionalism.

182. Dickerson, *supra* note 14, at 71, suggests that those who have not read a bill may have intended to adopt the intent

when particular bills are unimportant to legislators; they defer to those who care, in return for a similar deference in respect to matters about which they are most interested. Room also needs to be made for variations in weighting more subtle than complete delegation. A legislator may have considered an issue to some degree, but he may understand that his views, though they count, should count less than the views of those who have devoted more attention to the issue.

A variation on the theme of delegation claims not that legislators have chosen to delegate this precise authority to determine meaning by intention, but that they would choose to delegate this authority if they thought about it (particularly if they realized that they would receive in return reciprocal delegations for the subjects on which they are active and knowledgeable). This form of the idea of delegation relies on a hypothetical intent about the subject of which persons' mental states should count.

Finally, judges might regard "delegation" as a judicial doctrine (not depending on what legislators do or would think) that focuses on the intentions that will lead to the most sensible interpretation. If delegation comes down to principles of sensible interpretation as determined by judges, it varies little from the more bold assertion that the opinions of the few (or at least some few in especially influential positions) can count by themselves.

objectively manifested by the bill or the intent of those conversant with the language.

"Convention" lies close to ideas of delegation, but may shift to some degree the mental state that is taken as crucial for most members of a legislature. If conventions exist about who are authoritative spokespersons for the meaning of the language of a bill, and those persons ascribe particular meaning to language, others are taken to agree if they do not express themselves to the contrary. (A rather different conventions approach might eschew mental-state intentions, with judges taking certain statements as the basis for a finding of objective intent.) As with delegation, we might suppose that legislators actually subscribe to conventions and their significance, or that they would do so if they thought about them carefully. Under either of these versions, the ambiguous act of silence[183] is given the significance of assent. If the conventions about what constitutes agreement concern the actual mental states of legislators, the minimally required state of mind is subtly different from agreement or positive delegation. The state of mind a legislator has is one of acceptance of the meaning ascribed by the spokesperson as preferable to the alternative course of action available to the legislator. The legislator prefers to accept the statement about meaning as having authority to speak for him, rather than make the effort to develop and state a contrary view.

I have referred to this approach as one of convention, but we should be aware that natural conversational understandings here slide into artificial social

183.   *See* Radin, *supra* note 108, at 870–71.

conventions. In an informal context, if someone who makes a proposal goes on to say what she means by the proposal and her co-participants remain silent, they would ordinarily be taken to accept what she has said. If one of them later says to her, "The language of the proposal itself was unclear and I never accepted your gloss on it," she would reasonably respond, "If you didn't agree, why didn't you say so then? I took your silence as agreement." Of course, the effort that someone must make to form a judgment about the section of an obscure statute, to follow what spokespersons have said about it, and to express disagreement with their comments is much greater than the effort to disagree in ordinary conversation; and the natural inference from silence is accordingly much less. But the fundamental idea that what those responsible for a statute say about it has some special authority if it is not contradicted is not just some artificial convention about legislative practice. It is a lineal descendent of common conversational understandings.

I have thus far suggested that we cannot decide whose intentions within a legislature count, or how much they count, by simply reading off a conclusion from a basic theory of democratic government. That decision, rather, requires careful evaluation of the realities of the legislative process and of the way it works in relation to statutory interpretation.

II. Nonlegislators

Such an evaluation should also guide analysis of whether the intentions of any people other than legislators count. Imagine a system in which members of a separate executive branch are leaders of one of the two major political parties, and the legislators of the currently dominant party, without significant involvement in the way in which statutes are framed, vote faithfully for whatever bills the executive branch introduces.[184] It would be strange, indeed, to look exclusively to the opinions of legislators who blindly follow and pay little attention to what the proposing ministers believe they are accomplishing, without considering as relevant what the ministers understand. In cabinet systems of government (in which prime ministers and other ministers are also legislators) with two dominant parties and legislative voting according to party loyalty, the mental-state intentions of the ministers should probably count much more than those of any similar sized group of ordinary legislators, who have not participated actively in the formulation of statutory language or deliberations about its significance, and who vote for most government bills regardless of their own opinions on a subject.

184. This imaginary system differs from the United States in that legislators regularly follow what the executive leaders propose. The system differs from Great Britain and similar systems in which the executive leaders are also leaders within the legislature. The system also differs from various multiparty systems in which no single party is in a position to assure passage of its legislative program. This imaginary system may also differ from most existing systems of all types in the degree of passivity it assumes for legislators.

These comments are sufficient to suggest that when, in the United States, the executive branch introduces legislation that is adopted without much change, the intentions of the crucial members of that branch should count. In any real sense, they are an important part of the legislative process. One might explain the relevance of the views of members of the executive branch as based on a "delegation" by less well-informed legislators. The legislators' mental states would be that those of the executive drafters should have significance.[185]

The chief executive also figures formally in the legislative process with the power to veto, subject to a legislative override. The degree to which the president's (or governor's) understanding of statutory language should matter is reasonably arguable; but I believe this participation in the process is sufficient to give the executive's understanding some significance, at least if his views are expressed before the final vote of the legislature.[186]

The drafters of statutory language and staff members of legislators, who examine bills more closely than do the legislators themselves, also play

185. *See* Dickerson, *supra* note 14, at 72.

186. *Compare* Gasperini v. Center for Humanities, Inc., 518 U.S. 415, 424 (1996); United States v. Story, 891 F.2d 988, 993 (2d Cir. 1989), with Marc N. Harbert & Kurt A. Wimmer, "Presidential Signing Statements as Interpretations of Legislative Intent: An Executive Aggrandizement of Power," in 24 HARV J. ON LEGIS. 363 (1987). If the president's views are expressed only when he signs a bill into law, his comments are not subject to any response by legislators who disagree with his stated understanding. This is a good reason to give the comments little, if any, weight.

important parts in the process by which laws are enacted. As Stephen Breyer has emphasized, American legislatures have become progressively bureaucratized.[187] Formalism should not lead to a conclusion that only the views of actual legislators count, and even if one began with such a view, the intentions of drafters and other staffers might be drawn in by delegation from legislators.

The mental states of people who are not in the government, but have influence, should not have independent weight. Their role is less regularized than staffers, and they have neither been popularly elected nor appointed by elected officials. Their intentions should matter only insofar as they are accepted by people in the government. Because the intentions of outsiders should not be determinative, the required acceptance by insiders should be actual agreement with particular views, not merely some delegation to whatever views the outsiders happen to have.

One might reasonably draw a rough distinction among outsiders. Some are lobbyists pursuing particular policy objectives; others are organizations attempting to take a balanced approach to desirable legislation. The American Law Institute and the National Conference of Commissioners on Uniform State Laws are public institutions. (The Commissioners, but not the members of the A.L.I., are appointed by states.) Perhaps the opinions of those within such organizations who draft and approve model statutes should be treated like the opinions

187. *See* Breyer, *supra* note 58, at 858.

of drafters and staffers who work for the government. Certainly, officially expressed views that are contained in commentaries and available to legislators should be given weight, even when legislators are unlikely to have been aware of specific positions. I am inclined to think judges should not give weight to nongovernmental drafters' and sponsors' opinions that are indicated *informally* rather than officially expressed.

III. Conclusion

This chapter has argued for a flexible approach as to whose mental states should count and in what combinations, an approach that takes into account the realities of the legislative process. Minority understandings, standing alone, may have relevance and often may be tied to majorities by judgments of hypothetical intention, by delegation, and by convention. The views of those actively involved carry more weight than do those of fringe participants. Given the complexity of the modern legislative process, the understandings of legislative staffers and members of the executive branch who participate in formulating legislation may also have importance.

Most people who have written about mental-state intentions have assumed that, if interpreters of a law knew everything about the mental states of legislators, they should be able to fix upon the same single mental state and set combination of legislative actors as crucial in all instances. Difficulties in arriving at such conclusions have been taken as showing that a mental-state approach is wholly unworkable or should play a modest subsidiary role.[188] Any practical difficulties in determining mental states, then, merely add to more fundamental reasons not to accord mental states much weight.

Our examination has shown, somewhat surprisingly, that even if judges knew mental states of legislators fully, they should not have a uniform approach to which and whose mental states count. Of course, judges giving weight to probable mental states must implicitly arrive at conclusions about these matters in particular cases; but perhaps their intuitive calculations are so complex, they are understandably unable to state in formulaic terms just which and whose mental states are counting, and for exactly how much.

This ineradicable inarticulateness may seem odd, and one might take the absence of a simple formula as a powerful argument against judges using such a flexible approach. However, decisions of this sort are common for human choices. Suppose a mother consults all five of her children about what to do together on Saturday. If she does not reduce the question to a straight-out vote, but listens to each child's view and then decides what overall is best to do in terms of the children's expressed preferences, she may be hard put to say exactly why she has

188. *E.g.,* Dworkin, *supra* note 6, at 317–27 (wholly unworkable); Brest, *supra* note 36, at 221 (focusing on constitutional interpretation) (modest subsidiary role).

reached the conclusion she has. She can offer affirmative reasons for her decision, but may not be able to explain just why these reasons seemed stronger than those in favor of an alternative. The complexities of assessing relevant mental states, as well as the difficulties in discerning them, undoubtedly create opportunities for insincere judicial manipulation, but they may also underlie a more optimistic view that courts are capable of performing more perceptively than they can capture with formulas.[189]

If the analyses in this and the preceding chapter have been persuasive in their own terms, it remains open to reply that an interpretive process that genuinely gives weight to "mental-state intentions" encounters too many difficulties to make the exercise desirable. This line of objection awaits examination.

189. *See* Daniel A. Farber, "The Inevitability of Practical Reason: Statutes, Formalism, and the Rule of Law," 45 VAND. L. REV. 533 (1992). Farber has an interesting summary of empirical evidence about decisionmaking, *id.* at 554–58. For an eloquent claim that political decision depends on experienced judgment not reducible to abstract formulas, see Michael Oakeshott, *Rationalism in Politics and Other Essays* 7–13 (1962).

*

CHAPTER XI

DETERMINING MENTAL STATES

Questions 9[190] and 10[191] inquire about ways that judges can determine the mental states of legislators. The crucial, and sharply debated, issue of the place of legislative history in statutory interpretation is reserved for the next chapter. This chapter addresses what other sources may be used, and whether their use shows reliance on mental states. In both chapters, I simplify by assuming that the alternative to relying on legislators' mental states is to interpret statutory language as an ordinary (or expert) reader would understand it. The problems about discerning mental-state intentions alter only slightly if the alternatives one considers become more complex.

I. Uncontroversial Sources: How Far Do They Show Inquiry Into Mental States?

It helps to start with something that judges take into account in every common law jurisdiction. They may look at the preceding common law or

190. "How should courts discover relevant mental states?"

191. "Should courts make reference to aspects of legislative history, and, if so, on what basis?"

statutes that a new statute replaces and they can examine various public documents, like reports of independent commissions, to determine which problems needed to be fixed by enactment.[192] Judges interpret the new statute in light of that background. In some instances, judges give indecisive language a different reading than they would if they were to disregard that background. Our first question is whether reliance on that background is desirable; our second question is how we are to explain it.

As prior chapters have suggested, when someone in authority issues a directive, the recipient wants to know the problem to which the directive is addressed. If the parents talk to their teenage daughter about turning off the television, she will be sensitive to whether their past concern has been mainly about bedtime or the kinds of programs she watches. If they have let her go to bed when she pleases, but have closely monitored her programs, she will take their statement, "Go to bed at 11:00 when the 9:00 movie is over," as mainly an instruction not to watch other late programs. If she knows that their main concern has been bedtime, she will hear their statement differently. Interpreting directives with blindness to the problems they address would be ludicrous.[193] Judges should consider

192. *See, e.g.*, Dickerson, *supra* note 14, at 110, 161–62.

193. One *might* conclude, however, that allowing judges to focus attention on this subject would be unfair to primary addressees who happen to be unaware of the underlying problem.

background that illuminates underlying problems that statutes address.

Does use of this background show that mental-state intentions matter? An argument based on the background of prior law and commission reports might be formulated like this: "A major commission report shows that the perceived problem with existing law was x. The statute was aimed at that problem, and this unclear textual language furthers that objective by being interpreted in the following way." Or, to take another example, "The language of our penal code exactly replicates the Model Penal Code; the commentary to that code shows that such language is supposed to accomplish y." Words like "aimed," "objective," and "supposed to accomplish" sound like mental-state words.[194] If judges should try to discern mental-state intentions, these background sources are one method for doing so.

Can one sensibly approve of judicial use of these sources without endorsing inquiry into mental-state intentions? The answer is "yes," but it is less simple than sometimes has been supposed. An opponent of reliance on mental-state intentions might account for use of materials like commission reports in the following way: "The background helps to show how a reasonable reader, like the reasonable daughter in the T.V.-bedtime example, would understand an instruction. I have never said that every use of mental-state words is misguided. But

194. "Aimed" and "objective" emphasize purpose; "supposed to accomplish" in this context refers here to the specific coverage of a provision.

here we can think of the understanding of a typical reader, which is based on the likely objectives of a reasonable legislator passing a law against this background. We need not inquire about any actual mental states of actual legislators. Courts should not consider those." A reasonable reader who takes such background into account will interpret a statute in light of its aims, but that alone does not show that a court's use of prior law and independent reports makes actual mental states relevant.

An imaginary example tests the soundness of this response. In two 1890 towns, horses drawing carriages have injured pedestrians, and a number of horses have died from overexertion. Each town adopts an ordinance that says, "No carriage shall operate at more than twenty miles per hour." A court in 1910 faces the question of whether each law applies to automobiles. Although the judges recognize that the point is arguable, all are willing to apply the word "carriage" to automobiles if the danger to which each ordinance responds applies with roughly equal force to automobiles.[195] They do some research. The judges learn that, in Town 1, many people petitioned the council to safeguard those walking on the town streets, a report commissioned by the council recommended protective legislation, and winning council members ran on platforms of protecting the safety of streets. No one ever mentioned the welfare of horses. In Town 2, complaints about the need for a rule were directed

195. For discussion of "carriage" laws that might apply to automobiles, see Hart and Sacks, *supra* note 57, at 1183–85.

exclusively at the physical well-being of horses; no one ever mentioned pedestrian safety. In accordance with an approach that assigns significance to the problem being met, the court decides that the ordinance in Town 1 applies to automobiles and that the identically worded ordinance in Town 2 does not.

The court might conclude that a reasonable reader in Town 1 would take the ordinance as aimed at pedestrian safety, whereas a reasonable reader in Town 2 would take the ordinance as aimed at horse health. But why would a reasonable reader reach each conclusion? The readers would be considering the instructions as issuing from people in authority who are responding to particular problems. Like the teenage daughter, they would infer a purpose from the information about perceived difficulties. But any actual reader would not be thinking of a reasonable legislator; he or she would be thinking of council members who voted on the ordinance. If the judges phrase the question in terms of "reasonable readers" and "reasonable legislators," they abstract from actual readers and actual legislators, but the reasonable reader's reactions are based on what would be the likely purposes of most actual legislators in that position. Thus, we are drawn back to the probable mental-state intentions of people who issue instructions in response to complaints. When statutory language might be supported by various purposes, reference to the social problem being fixed does not avoid reliance on mental-state intentions altogether. Assigning mental states to a reasonable legislator requires some sense of the way in which legislators typically (or ideally) react to dangers they perceive.

If the "reasonable reader" strategy does not avoid all reliance on mental states of legislators, it may successfully avoid inquiry into the particular mental states of individuals. One could construct the reasonable reader here as someone who infers a purpose held by members of the council in general, or members voting for the measure, or most members voting for the measure, or a reasonable council member, without distinguishing the intentions of some legislators from those others.[196] The reasonable reader might not try to figure out what anyone actually thought on a particular occasion. This is the manner in which judges use commission reports and prior law. They do not distinguish between various influences on particular legislators. Judges treat these materials as if they guide legislators equally. So long as a particular source of interpretation fails to provide a basis for distinguishing the intentions of some legislators from the intentions of

196. I use the word "construct" because an interpreter will conceive a reasonable reader in line with what the interpreter thinks is the desirable way to interpret; there is no single version of "reasonable reader" that dictates a method of interpretation. Since, in any complex society, readers of different backgrounds will have somewhat different understandings (*see* Dickerson, *supra* note 14, at 116), the construction of a typical or reasonable reader may involve worries about precise mental states and of how to combine the mental states of various individual readers. These worries are not so unlike those that arise over legislative intentions. I explore these matters in more detail in "Are Mental States Relevant for Statutory and Constitutional Interpretation?," *supra* note 152.

others, no one may need to decide whether these sources are relevant because they illuminate actual mental states, or the hypothetical mental state of a reasonable legislator, or the understanding of a reasonable reader apprised of the information the sources provide.

II.   Disfavored Sources of Possible Guidance

Some possible techniques of determining statutory meaning are strongly disfavored. Lawyers cannot call legislators to testify about what they had in mind, although California courts allow affidavits by legislators about the intent of the legislature as a whole.[197] In general, judges do not consider what legislators say after legislation is adopted (for example, in a book or public lecture). Without doubt, judges should be suspicious of anything said after the event, outside the legislative process. But is that a sufficient reason to disregard such statements altogether?

People's statements after an event, about what they were trying to accomplish, are often revealing. If virtually absolute preclusion is to be justified, it must be because admitting a source of knowledge is impractical or unfair—because the source is too easily subject to prejudicial manipulation or is comparatively unavailable for citizens—or because the record for interpretation needs to be set at the time

197.   Rich v. State Bd. of Optometry, 235 Cal. App. 2d 591, 603, 45 Cal. Rptr. 512 (1965).

of enactment. Impracticality can explain why legislators are not called to testify; legislators should not have to drop their primary business whenever any litigant thinks their testimony would be useful. Most post-enactment statements are easily subject to manipulation; other legislators are not then in a position to disagree about what was meant. The primary problem of unavailability is that sources should not be used against a citizen unless they are conveniently available to him or her. The question is not just of pure access—an interview in *Time* magazine is more widely available than a commission report. The issue is also one of regularity. A client or lawyer needs to know where to look for information; the places in which statements outside the process may appear are incredibly diverse. Of course, an extra wrinkle in the problem of unavailability occurs if the clarifying statement appears after the crucial legal events have occurred; neither party could conceivably have been aware of such a statement before acting.

The concern about a complete record is twofold. If the record can change after enactment, it follows that the best interpretation also may change. Whether changes in best interpretations are desirable, or even tolerable, is a subject sharply put by various post-enactment events. I turn to that topic in Chapters Fifteen through Nineteen.

The other concern is narrower: Should any understandings count if they were not available to other legislators at the time? Even if one accepts a legislator's post-enactment statement as honestly reflective of his understanding when a bill was passed, it could have had no direct influence on other legislators if not expressed. (Informal oral comments at the time could have affected *some* legislators.) Various inferences, from the mental states of one legislator to the mental states of others, are greatly weakened if the legislator's mental state was unspoken. In various nonlegal examples (in particular, the tutor who was told to teach the children about religion), I have indicated that the mental state of someone issuing instructions may count for interpretation even if not revealed until subsequent to the instructions themselves. I have also suggested that the mental states of legislators can count even if they do not approach a majority. It may seem to follow that mental states not expressed until after enactment must be able to count for *something*. However, perhaps they count for so little that judges are justified in disregarding them. And, as a matter of principle, one may believe that the formalities of the legislative process should entail that evidence of intent be at least available to the legislature (or one house of the legislature) when it votes for a bill. On such a view, the only evidences of mental states that judges should consider are manifestations prior to enactment.

The next chapter asks whether courts appropriately consider what takes place within the legislative process. If they do not, they should certainly not pay attention to post-enactment statements made outside the legislative process. Even if judges should consult legislative history, they should be very skeptical about the circumstances of post-enactment remarks. An ideal judge would not automatically disregard them all completely; but interpretive practice that precludes consideration of such remarks is a reasonable way to simplify determinations of meaning by excluding highly peripheral and manipulable data.

III. Conclusion

Judges consistently consider some sources for understanding statutory provisions beyond the text itself. These include the preceding law and reports of independent commissions highlighting problems that need to be addressed. The use of those sources may be conceived as helping to reveal mental-state understandings of legislators, but their use can also be justified under methods that eschew inquiry into the subjective intentions of actual legislators.

Various post-enactment indications of previous understandings are widely disfavored. Whether these should have any role at all is reasonably debatable.

CHAPTER XII

THE APPROPRIATE PLACE OF LEGISLATIVE HISTORY

I. Legislative History and Its Use

This chapter discusses the use of legislative history and possible justifications for that use, the issues posed by Question 10.[198] By "legislative history," I refer to the record of the internal workings of the legislative process, including hearings, committee reports, statements on the floor of the legislature, and messages accompanying presidential signatures. The legislative history also includes comparisons of the final language of an act with the language of previous drafts.

During most of this century, use of legislative history has flourished. According to James Landis, "The records of legislative assemblies once opened and read with a knowledge of legislative procedure often reveal the richest kind of evidence [of the meaning a representative assembly attached to statutory words]."[199] In *United States v. American*

198. "Should courts make reference to aspects of legislative history, and, if so, on what basis?"

199. Landis, *supra* note 112, at 888.

171

Trucking Ass'n, Justice Reed wrote for the Supreme Court, "When aid to construction of the meaning of words, as used in the statute, is available, there certainly can be no 'rule of law' which forbids its use, however clear the words may appear on 'superficial examination.' "[200] In 1983, Judge Patricia Wald reported that the Supreme Court had examined legislative history in nearly every statutory case it had addressed the previous term and concluded, "No occasion for statutory construction now exists when the Court will not look at the legislative history."[201]

In recent years, judges and scholars have debated whether judges should use legislative history. Justice Scalia has been the most prominent and influential opponent of that reliance, writing that "legislative history should not be used as an authoritative indication of a statute's meaning."[202] Judges and scholars have often supposed that *if* legislative history counts for interpretation, it is because it reveals the mental-state intentions of legislators; but others, including Ronald Dworkin, have presented

200. 310 U.S. 534 (1940).

201. Wald, "Some Observations on the Use of Legislative History in the 1981 Supreme Court Term," 68 IOWA L. REV. 195, 195 (1983).

202. *See, e.g.,* Scalia, *supra* note 4, at 29–30. *See also id.* 29–37. However, Justice Scalia accepts the use of legislative history to confirm that an absurd disposition was not intended. Green v. Bock Laundry Mach. Co., 490 U.S. 504, 527 (1989) (Scalia, J., concurring). As Stephen Breyer has pointed out, *supra* note 58, at 850, 852–53, Scalia has actually accepted legislative history in some other rare cases.

alternative accounts to justify its use.[203] I shall first consider using legislative history to discern intentions, and then address some alternative proposals.

Some pieces of legislative history are more revealing than others of what many legislators, and the most important legislators, think. Conference committee reports, written after differences in language between the two houses of Congress have been ironed out, have the highest status in the United States. These indicate the understanding of the members from both houses of Congress who are most closely associated with a bill. Committee reports from the House and Senate are next in importance. These reflect the work of the committees that have deliberated about legislation and that are mainly responsible for the language adopted by each house. These reports also may help other legislators understand what a bill is about. Judges give statements on the floor of Congress significant weight only if they are made by committee chairpersons or others shepherding a bill toward passage. Statements by opponents taken by themselves are treated as irrelevant. I have suggested that what opponents believe is much less important than what supporters believe; moreover, opponents often attribute undesirable or highly controversial meaning to language, in order to emphasize the danger of proposed legislation. What witnesses say in hearings is also generally regarded as irrelevant, unless that

203. Dworkin, *supra* note 6, at 342–47. It is worth mentioning that one *might* add other reasons for using legislative history to a mental-states account. These reasons would then be a supplement to that account, rather than an alternative.

is the obvious trigger for some crucial change in the language of a bill.[204]

How instructive are changes made in the content of bills as they move through the legislature? Max Radin commented that successive drafts give "us little information about the final form, since we never really know why one gave way to any other."[205] James Landis responded that substitution of new language "necessarily involves an element of choice often leaving little doubt as to the reasons governing such a choice."[206] In truth, much depends on circumstances. Occasionally, a substitution of new language is revealing;[207] often it tells very little.

William Eskridge has recently ranked sources in legislative history in the following way: "Committee Reports, Sponsor/Floor Manager Statements, Re-

204. *See* Securities and Exch. Comm'n v. Robert Collier & Co., 76 F.2d 939, 940 (2d Cir. 1935). Perhaps a statement by a highly authoritative witness, such as the head of an executive department that has drafted a bill, should carry some weight, even if no change in language is made. Perhaps also consistent statements by witnesses of highly diverse persuasions should combine to have some force for the understanding of legislators. A different kind of reliance on witnesses' statements is to understand the social circumstances at which a law is directed. In Huddleston v. United States, 415 U.S. 814, 829 (1974), the Court relied in part on congressional testimony of the President of the Pawnbrokers' Association of the City of New York for an account of how pawnbrokers deal with guns.

205. Radin, *supra* note 108, at 873.

206. Landis, *supra* note 112, at 889.

207. *See, e.g.*, the circumstances in Securities and Exch. Comm'n v. Robert Collier & Co., 76 F.2d 939 (2d Cir. 1935).

jected Proposals, Floor and Hearing Colloquy, Non-legislator Statements, Legislative Inaction, Subsequent History."[208]

The connection between pieces of legislative history and the likely mental states of legislators has shifted over time. In 1893, Congress adopted the Railway Safety Appliances Act, discussed in Chapter Five.[209] The language was ambiguous about whether railway cars, equipped with automatic couplers, had to be able to couple with each other.[210] Earlier draft language had clearly required this operating compatibility between couplers. Each time the language was changed in the Senate, the proposer indicated that he did not intend to alter the requirement of compatibility; and the committee chairman, doubtful about one such change, stated that he accepted as the sense of the Senate that no alteration in compatible coupling was intended.[211] One who reads the records of the Senate floor debates senses that a high percentage of members were present and paying attention to the discussion. The final vote in favor of the act was fairly one-sided. It is *conceivable* that many silent senators did not

208. Eskridge, *supra* note 86, at 222.

209. *See* Johnson v. Southern Pac. Co., 196 U.S. 1 (1904).

210. The crucial language of Section 2 was this: "[I]t shall be unlawful for any such common carrier to haul or permit to be hauled or used on its line any car used in moving interstate traffic not equipped with couplers coupling automatically by impact, and which can be uncoupled without the necessity of men going between the ends of the cars."

211. 24 CONG. REC. S1331–1333 (Feb. 8, 1893); 1371–1372 (Feb. 9, 1893); *see especially* 1371 (52nd Congress, 2d Session, Senate debates).

suppose they were insisting upon compatible coupling, but no one spoke up to that effect. The reasonable conclusion is that most of those voting for (and against) the act assumed that it did require compatible coupling.

Few, if any, recent debates could generate such confidence. Most floor debates are sparsely attended; legislators have little time for the details of legislation; and the amount and detail of legislation is vastly greater than it was one hundred years ago. Committee reports may not be read by most committee members, much less other legislators. They are written by staff members, with some suggestions from private lobbyists; and their main readership within the legislative process is other staffers.

About most litigated issues, realism compels recognition that few members of Congress will have a specific intention on the matter. Either judges should not rely on specific intentions, or they should implicitly accept notions that assign importance to the mental states of key committee members, and perhaps staff. These substantial difficulties help render plausible the position that judges should not concern themselves with mental-state intentions; and students who have worked as legislative assistants are often the most skeptical about reliance on legislative history and mental-state intentions. But are these doubts themselves sufficient to overcome a preliminary presumption, based on the analysis of the last three chapters, that internal evidence about what legislators had in mind may be valuable for interpreting what they did?

II. Arguments Against Use of Legislative History

A number of arguments have been made against using legislative history as a guide to mental-state intentions of legislators. I consider, in turn, claims that: (1) legislators enact statutes, not legislative history; (2) legislative history is insufficiently accessible or of little value; (3) the history is too easily subject to manipulation or misperception; (4) its use breeds poor drafting and irresponsible legislative activity; (5) constitutional values preclude legislatures' effectively delegating responsibility for statutory meaning to subgroups of legislators.

A. Legislators Enact Statutes

The claim that legislators enact statutes, not legislative history, may or may not be an independent argument. If this claim merely restates with rhetorical force a conclusion that, overall, mental-state intentions and legislative history should not figure in interpretation, it is a plausible position, but one I finally reject. Sometimes the argument is presented differently—as a self-evident truth. It is undeniable that what legislators enact is the statutory language, and this gives the language a special place. However, most legislators no more read the details of statutory language than they read committee reports. In many circumstances, people who are subject to directives rightly interpret them according to what the person(s) who issued them had in mind.[212] There is no simple reason to suppose that statutes in general should be different, although we have explored some strong reasons why text should receive primary emphasis in statutory interpretation. We need now to see if some less-than-simple reasons establish that legislative history should be barred from consideration.

B.   *Accessibility and Value*

The difficulty of acquiring knowledge of relevant legislative history could be one reason for judges to give it no or little weight. In general, judges should not rely heavily on information that is not practically accessible to the main addressees of statutes, given the time and expense one could reasonably expect them to undertake.[213] In the past, some pieces of legislative history may have been hard to get,[214] but this problem has been largely eliminated by computerization. Although lawyers doing modest research may still not have time to scour the legislative history, the crucial question now is not whether

212.   The previous chapters establish that such interpretation *may* be appropriate even when the author of a directive can obligate the recipient only by issuing a directive.

213.   One could expect more extensive legal research if the main addressees were large corporations than if they were ordinary, private people. Dickerson, *supra* note 14, at 150–51, points out that it is very difficult for someone to search the legislative history for all that might be relevant before a dispute arises.

214.   *See, e.g.*, Justice Robert Jackson's opinion in United States v. Public Util. Comm'n of Calif., 345 U.S. 295, 319–320 (1953) (Jackson, J., concurring). *But see* Elizabeth Finley, "Crystal Gazing: The Problem of Legislative History," 45 A.B.A .J. 1281 (1959).

lawyers can find legislative history, but what it is worth in comparison with the research effort, time, and client expense that is required if lawyers are to review it.

Research efforts will be unprofitable if legislative history rarely reveals anything relevant. The danger of "coming up empty" is greater if one is looking for specific opinions about the force of operative language that bear on a narrow problem the court is facing than if one seeks broader purposes or further intentions. Any committee report will say something about the purposes of a bill; and most legislators are likely to have some sense of a major statute's aims, even if they are unfamiliar with its details.

On many occasions, the danger is not that lawyers and judges will find nothing relevant in the legislative history, but that what they find will be indecisive, some materials helping one side, some helping the other. Just how useful legislative history can be is a practical question that those with extensive experience can best resolve. Anyone's judgment on this subject should be based on the wide range of cases resolved by courts and agencies. Focus on the particularly difficult cases that the U.S. Supreme Court takes may be seriously misleading. On the basis of the divergent evaluations one finds in judicial opinions and professional literature, I believe that the value of legislative history is worth the costs of its examination. As Stephen Breyer suggests, the use of legislative history often enough "helps appellate courts reach interpretations that tend to make the law itself more coherent, workable, or fair...."[215]

C. Manipulation or Misperception

The worry about manipulation or misperception is a graver concern than the simple concern that value may not justify cost. There are actually two worries about manipulation. The more straightforward one is that legislative history increases opportunities for judicial manipulation, that judges who review that history will behave like people "looking over a crowd and picking out [their] friends," as Harold Leventhal said.[216] Just how far judges manipulate different standards of interpretation is subject to argument. When I review judicial opinions, I see what are either surprising, counterintuitive assessments or self-conscious manipulations of *all* standards of interpretation. Opinions are often devoted to making results appear objective and compelled by law, although the results are not so objective and not so compelled by law. In one respect, manipulation of legislative history may be more dangerous than manipulation of text; it is harder for the critic to spot, especially if he does not have a dissenting opinion or opposing brief to put against the opinion. But the idea that judges, in general, are *more* manipulative of legislative history than other standards of interpretation has yet to be persuasively argued, and it is not easy to see just how one

215. Breyer, *supra* note 58 at 847.

216. *See* Wald, *supra* note 201, at 214 (quoting from private conversation).

could establish that one method of interpretation lends itself to greater manipulation than another.

Even if judges are not self-consciously manipulative, they may misperceive the force of the legislative history, treating it in an unjustified, one-sided way. The volume and heterogeneity of the sources of legislative history raise particular dangers that judges will find that the history supports their own predispositions or fits the account of the lawyer who has made the better argument.[217]

The deeper worry about manipulation concerns the legislative level, with judges playing unwitting dupes to clever legislators, staffers, and lobbyists. The worry goes something like this: So long as legislative history was compiled for use within the legislative branch, it remained relatively untainted. But everyone has long since discovered that the history is now important, perhaps mainly important, for judges who interpret laws. This creates a powerful incentive to stack the legislative history. If one wants a particular result, it is much easier to insert language in a committee report than to alter the language of a statute. Legislators and staffers, typically when induced by lobbyists, will add language to legislative history to achieve results they seek, thus bypassing the formal processes of statutory adoption and warping the history so that it is unreflective of general intentions.

217. Adrian Vermuele, *supra* note 61, argues that problems of judicial competence in evaluating legislative history are so severe, one should oppose its use even if one thinks legislators' intentions should count for interpretation.

Without doubt, the incentives portrayed in this account, and thus the dangers, do exist. But how commonly are these dangers realized? Here, it is not enough to rely on "public choice" theory, which hypothesizes that legislators pursue their narrow self-interest and will take whatever opportunity they have, in order to further the wishes of supporters who can help ensure re-election. Public choice theory may help explain some behavior, but it is not, and has never claimed to be, an overall description of human motivation.[218] As Peter Strauss and Einer Elhauge have urged, insofar as the behavioral explanations of public choice theory are valid, they must apply to judges as well as to legislators, in which event almost any efforts to constrain judicial interpretation become useless exercises.[219] Further, if one assumes that legislators and staffers are on the lookout for opportunities to salt the legislative history, their opponents presumably are aware of this risk and will either prevent misleading language or counter it with their own disavowals or competing bits of misleading history.

No one can tell us what the incidence is of manipulation of legislative history on the basis of anecdote and a priori public choice analysis. Perhaps the abuses are now frequent, and perhaps committee chairs and others have a power that opponents

218. *See generally* Daniel Farber and Philip Frickey, *supra* note 163.

219. Strauss, "Comment: Legal Process and Judges in the Real World," 12 CARDOZO L. REV 1653, 1658 (1991); Elhauge, "Does Interest Group Theory Justify More Intrusive Judicial Review?" 101 Yale L. J. 31, 85 (1991).

cannot often counter; but the case for this needs to be made on the basis of convincing empirical study that has yet to be done.[220]

D. Incompetent Performance

Does judicial use of legislative history breed poor drafting and irresponsible legislative activity? If courts concentrate on text to the exclusion of history, perhaps legislators will be more careful about drafting and will refrain, during the process of enactment, from adopting novel language that has not been carefully reviewed. In some countries, notably Great Britain, in which legislative history plays virtually no interpretive role, drafting is much more careful; but it is hard to trace cause and effect because of drastic differences among political systems. In Great Britain, party loyalty ensures a much smoother trip from proposal to passage than that to which most American legislation is subject. In the United States, important amendments often take place in midstream, without careful scrutiny of the way a new provision fits with the rest of the package. Further, extensive drafting efforts are "wasted" on the high percentage of bills that never get adopted.

No matter how careful drafters are, they will fail to foresee many situations, and the statutory language they choose will fail to resolve some situations that they do foresee, because they will be inattentive to an aspect of the language they have chosen, or will self-consciously decide not to settle a

220. *See* Frickey, *supra* note 84, at 255.

sore issue. If the legislative history can help judges resolve such cases in accord with the aims of legislators, that is a strong argument for its use, even if the cost is marginally less care in legislative drafting.

E. *Constitutional Considerations*

John Manning has recently made a strong argument for textualism that does not rely fundamentally on poor legislative drafting or willful manipulation of legislative history. He claims that, at its core, interpretive use of legislative history offends the separation of powers because it delegates to one part of the legislature the authority to say what a statute means.[221] It allows legislators, through the use of legislative history, to bypass the requirements of bicameralism and presentment to the President. Manning's objection may have special force when legislators self-consciously employ legislative history to resolve statutory meaning for the executive branch and the judiciary; but he believes judicial reliance on that history is inappropriate even when legislators are honestly trying to inform each other about what they are enacting. Manning does not deny that legislative history may give us a good idea of the aims of many legislators; nonetheless it should be disregarded because it is not law made in the way that law within our system is supposed to be made. This is not merely a formal matter. Bicameralism and executive veto were de-

221. John Manning, "Textualism as a Nondelegation Doctrine," 97 COLUM. L. REV. 673 (1997).

signed, and function, to prevent hasty, ill-considered statutes. The safeguard they provide is sidestepped when authoritative meaning is established by legislative history.

The strength of Manning's attack on legislative history is the subject of practical evaluation, not knock-down conceptual analysis. Insofar as the concern is presidential signature and bicameralism, some pieces of legislative history are more vulnerable than others. If the report comes from a conference committee, or parallel reports of committees in both houses take a similar position, then bicameralism is satisfied. If the President expresses agreement in his signing message, then we have legislative history that represents all three government organs that must approve ordinary legislation. Manning would answer that, even then, the pieces of legislative history have not been formally approved.

But how significant is formal approval, by itself, when we know that neither the President (nor his staff) nor most legislators (nor their staffs) carefully review the actual language of many statutes they adopt? In reality, they may be guided more by items of legislative history explaining what a bill does than by the detailed language of provisions themselves. Most legislators may delegate to colleagues on committees and to staff the details of *statutory language* as much as they delegate the authority to create legislative history.

Manning's argument is at its most powerful when courts rely on a committee report or the deliberations of one chamber. Of course, even then these materials may influence members of the other chamber and the President; but if use of such legislative history comes close to delegating to members of one chamber the ability to legislate, then the tension with the constitutional process of legislation is most severe.

In order to respond to Manning's worry on this score, one may distinguish between authoritative instruction and explanation, rely on some theory of endorsement, or claim that a limited sacrifice in realization of principles of separation of powers and nondelegation is justified by practical need.

Let me take the last two responses together. Not every useful explanation of what a statute does belongs in a preamble. Draft laws, such as the Uniform Commercial Code and the Model Penal Code, often have substantial commentaries. If the operating codes based on a model vary from state to state, these state codes usually have separate commentaries. Judges do not hesitate to refer to the various commentaries to interpret the codes. If the commentaries are approved by the same process as the codes themselves, Manning has no objection to their use. Yet very few people in the legislative branch will have read the commentaries. A vote hardly enhances each point made in a commentary; rather, a vote expresses confidence that the process producing the commentaries fairly reflects what the statutory language is designed to achieve.

Why not have a similar approval of legislative history tagged onto a statute? A law might say, for example, "Positions developed in traditionally influential aspects of the legislative history shall be taken as indicating the meaning of the provisions of this statute." *If* a simple statute could successfully endorse legislative history, then one might suppose that a single law could endorse use of legislative history for all future statutes, thus avoiding the necessity of passing such language in each instance. If that process would satisfy Manning, then his practical worry could be met by a law or laws approving use of legislative history. And, if explicit approval would suffice, one can argue that Congress and the President have implicitly approved this strategy of interpretation by long acceptance.[222]

Since Manning analogizes use of legislative history to explicit delegation to a subgroup of legislators and to a legislative veto procedure, each adopted by a full statutory process,[223] he would, presumably, not permit any form of statutory endorsement to justify otherwise unacceptable judicial use of discrete pieces of legislative history not themselves formally adopted by vote.[224] But if we take this

222. Muriel Morisey Spence, "The Sleeping Giant: Textualism as Power Struggle," 67 So CAL L. REV. 585, 615–18 (1994), suggests ways in which Congress may affirm legislative history.

223. Manning, *supra* note 221, at 715–17.

224. Starting from the view that legislation is to be interpreted according to ordinary principles of communication, Dickerson, *supra* note 14 at 262–80, believes that virtually all effects to establish special techniques of interpretation for the future should be regarded as ineffective. This position is too restrictive

"hard line about endorsement," we face a serious difficulty. If legislative history is otherwise useful for interpreting legislation, and what is contained in legislative history cannot comfortably be developed elsewhere, should it be barred from consideration? Even if Manning's proposal better carries out some ideal of separation of powers, nevertheless some sacrifice may be warranted in the interests of coherent law and sensible law creation.[225] Manning suggests that any useful explanation can be enacted into law.[226] Certainly one crucial question about whether a move toward textualism is desirable is whether legislative history performs an appropriate function that cannot be equally served in some other way.

This brings us to the difference between authoritative instruction and explanation. Manning writes as if courts may be giving explanations in legislative history the same kind of authority as statutory language. If history and language are otherwise not distinguishable, his nondelegation point is forceful. Neither Congress as a whole nor the courts could allow a committee to write authoritative statutory language that was not adopted by Congress and the President. It follows that no one can authorize committees to determine meaning in committee reports that are not adopted by Congress as a whole.

of a legislature's ability to influence techniques of interpretation for future statutes that do not themselves address interpretive methods.

225. *See* Mistretta v. United States, 488 U.S. 361, 371–372 (1989).

226. Manning, *supra* note 221, at 729–30.

In response, Peter Strauss draws a sharp distinction between statutory language and legislative history:[227] Judges *must* take account of the former; in their discretion, they *may* take account of the latter. On this understanding, judges are "not *bound* by legislative history,"[228] as they are by statutory language. I am sympathetic with Strauss's attempt to distinguish explanation from authoritative instruction, but I am uncomfortable with his precise way of putting it. If judges *should* consult legislative history, and if a particular history overwhelmingly supports one conclusion in a case that is otherwise very close, I think judges are bound to decide in that way—they are not free just to disregard the compelling force of the legislative history.

Instructions that are unclear in context should usually be interpreted in accordance with what those who issued them had in mind, if that can be ascertained.[229] When instructions are issued corpo-

227. Peter Strauss, "The Courts and the Congress: Should Judges Disdain Political History?" 98 COLUM L. REV. 242 (1998). James Brudney, in "Congressional Commentary on Judicial Interpretation of Statutes: Idle Chatter or Telling Response?" 93 MICH L. REV. 1, 42 (1994), says legislative history is not "law," but is consulted as are other sources of interpretation outside the statutory text.

228. Strauss, *supra* note 227, at 250. Dickerson adopts a somewhat similar position. For him legislative history should not count at all when judges exercise their cognitive function of discovering meaning; when judges act creatively in respect to issues not resolved by a statute, they may consider some legislative history. Dickerson, *supra* note 14 at 156–57, 169.

229. I make this assertion, subject to reservations I expressed in respect to mental-state intentions in previous chapters and subject to other reservations I discuss below.

rately by a combination of organizations of many persons, the intentions of issuing members in each organization count for something, even if they do not represent the intentions of members of other organizations. Such use of intentions to understand instructions does not violate a principle that each organization must formally approve the instructions themselves. What I have said does provide *some* basis for distinguishing intentions from formal instructions; but it alone is not a full answer to Manning's position. His point is that bicameralism and presentment are *most respected* if only legislative actions that pass those formal hurdles receive interpretive consideration. Nevertheless, a slight sacrifice in maximum effect for those requisites is warranted in order to achieve reasonable governance.

F.   Crucial Questions

I have discussed a number of arguments against judges using legislative history to provide evidence of mental-state intentions, which in turn guides interpretation of the meaning of statutory provisions. I have not found any of these sufficiently powerful to undermine the traditional use of legislative history. Even if none alone does so, perhaps the arguments together show that this use of legislative history is unwarranted or unwise. In this respect, I believe there are three critical questions: (1) How widespread is manipulative, misleading creation of legislative history within the legislative branch?; (2) How able are judges to sift the wheat from the chaff, i.e., to rely on nonmanipulative legislative history and to reject its manipulative cousin, and to perceive fairly the force of various items of legislative history?; (3) Could procedures that involve formal approval of explanatory material yield the major benefits of legislative history, across the range of circumstances in which that history is now used for interpretation, *without* imposing undue costs on actors in the legislative process? If I became persuaded that manipulative creation of legislative history is very common, that judges cannot separate wheat from chaff, and that the benefits of explanatory materials typically can be well achieved by a process that makes all of Congress more accountable, I would agree with the critics who contend that use of legislative history should come to an end.

At present, my conclusion is somewhat different. Overall, judges should give less weight to legislative history as revealing mental-state intentions than would once have been appropriate. They should be realistic about whose mental-state intentions count and why, and they should be very cautious about moving from any piece of legislative history to mental-state intentions. But explanations that are not easily subject to formal approval play a useful role in interpretation. Judges should not abandon altogether either legislative history or reference to mental-state intentions.

III. Alternative Accounts

Alternative accounts of the use of legislative history assign it some importance but without tying pieces of that history to mental-state intentions. Manning has suggested that textualist judges may use legislative history to supply objective, unmanufactured evidence of a statute's context.[230] Judges interpreting statutes would treat the legislative history in the manner that an appellate judge regards an opinion by a trial court judge.[231] Ronald Dworkin has urged that one reason why judges may consult legislative history is that it provides a sense of attitudes outside the legislature.[232] Since what committee reports and members of Congress say about the significance of pieces of legislation is a much more reliable indication of what members of Congress and their staffs believe than what people outside the legislature believe, it is a bit odd to assign legislative history weight as to the latter and not the former. But the oddity might be justified if one had strong enough independent reasons to conclude that the mental states of members of the population matter and that the mental states of legislators do not.[233]

230. Manning, *supra* note 221, at 731.

231. *Id.* at 732.

232. Dworkin, *supra* note 6 at 347, 349. If public attitudes count as part of the relevant statutory context, use of legislative history to discover such attitudes might be a subcategory of Manning's idea of legitimate uses.

233. To be fair, Dworkin says the general attitudes of the population are what are relevantly revealed, not their specific intentions or even their sense of the purposes of a particular statute. *Id.* at 349. This distinction makes his account more plausible than it would otherwise be.

These two proposed uses of legislative history are reasonable, whatever one concludes about using that history to reveal the legislators' mental-state intentions. If one believes in using history to discern mental-state intentions, these uses can be supplementary; if one rejects using history to discern mental-state intentions, these uses can be alternatives. These uses alone would be unlikely to give legislative history anything close to the importance it has in a mental-states account.

A use that initially appears as a more direct competitor to a mental-states account is that pieces of legislative history do have authoritative status in explaining statutory provisions, but the authoritative status is a matter of convention. According to Dworkin, for example, practice assigns particular items, such as committee reports, a role in explaining why a statute was adopted.[234] Rejecting any search for mental-state intentions, Dworkin claims, instead, that courts should consider Congress as a single body acting through time. Statutory language should be interpreted to fit with what else the legislature has done, and with the rest of the corpus of law. Legislative history has the status that it does

234. For Dworkin, the weight judges should assign to legislative history diminishes as time passes from the adoption of the statute. Thus, a court should pay less attention to the legislative history of an old statute than to that of a new one. This view, standing alone, could fit well enough with one particular view that legislative history aids the search for mental-state intentions—a view that emphasizes purpose and gives specific intentions diminishing significance over time. *See* Dworkin, *supra* note 6, at 348–50.

only because convention assigns it an explanatory place and because it well reflects public attitudes.

No doubt, some conventions about legislative history have arisen, though current Supreme Court justices disagree about its use. Thought about how exactly those conventions have arisen, and how they might change, provides one test of a conventional approach that competes with a mental-states approach. The most straightforward reason why particular pieces of legislative history have the most weight is that they have best reflected the ideas— the mental-state intentions—of the members, especially those members who have carefully considered a statute's language.

Let us reconsider the example of the speed limit on carriages, and imagine that the city council had been pressed both by people concerned about pedestrian safety and by people concerned about the welfare of horses to adopt such an ordinance. One legislator introduces the bill in order to impose a speed limit. He says, "I believe the concern about horses is absolutely ridiculous, but I want to protect our children." Three of the eight other legislators make similar remarks. Five of the members of the council remain silent but vote for the law. On this record, it is natural to suppose that, if the others wanted mainly to protect horses, they probably would have said *something* about that objective. If this record were available to it,[235] a court would draw from the remarks of the supporters the con-

235. Relevant legislative history is typically not available for local ordinances in the United States.

clusion that the legislators wanted to protect children, not horses. By contrast, if the justification for using legislative history lies in convention, a judge might assign weight to the explanation of the sponsor because that has been the traditional practice, not because of a connection between the sponsor's statements and anyone's actual beliefs.

The weight that is actually assigned to various pieces of legislative history is almost certainly to be explained by their perceived connection to mental-state intentions. Someone who thinks conventions about legislative history are useful, but that reliance on mental-state intentions has always been misguided, must conclude that the notions about respective weight have arisen because of some misconception of the importance of mental states.[236] This account is more awkward than one that finds the actual justification for a convention in the perceived reasons that gave rise to it.

236. One could believe, instead, that convention now gives committee reports, etc. a certain kind of status that is not based on a connection to mental-state intentions, even though their initial acquisition of that status was based on a justified belief about such a connection. A holder of this view could believe that a previously existent and significant connection to intentions has disappeared, in which event convention would now take the place that formerly was occupied by the connection. But Dworkin's view appears to be that reliance on mental-state intentions has always been a mistake, if, in fact, it has ever existed. Thus, he must think either that any connection to mental states was insufficiently strong to explain reliance on pieces of legislative history or that, even though some pieces of legislative history happen to connect strongly to such intentions, reliance on them never would have been justified on that basis.

What of possible changes in conventions? Suppose convincing empirical work showed that neither members of Congress nor their staff read committee reports, and that the reports typically represent the unreviewed efforts of one or two staffers who are influenced by private lobbyists. On the mental-states account, this revelation should greatly lower the value of committee reports. Indeed, similar, though less extreme, factual premises are offered against judges using legislative history at all, or against their giving it as much weight as they have in the past. I have indicated that the latter position is persuasive.

Were the use of legislative history warranted independent of any ability to reflect legislators' mental-state intentions, the history's increasing failure to reflect those intentions would not call for reduced weight. If one believes that a diminishing connection between pieces of that history and the perceptions of legislators and staff *should* lead to a reduction in their weight, that suggests strongly that the justifiable use of legislative history connects more powerfully to mental-state intentions than pure conventionalist theory allows.[237]

Various positions about legislative history fall between a mental-states approach and a pure conventionalist account. One position emphasizes that

237. Someone can, of course, acknowledge that conventions of this sort change, but it is doubtful whether a diminishing connection to the beliefs of legislators should cause such a change. An alternative explanation for shifts in the force of particular pieces of legislative history might look to what a reasonable legislator *should* use to inform himself.

items of legislative history, like earlier reports of independent commissions that generate legislative proposals, are useful to indicate what problems Congress is addressing. This relatively modest role for legislative history need not make reference to any particular legislator's mental-state intentions, but it does concern the reasons why some legislators (or reasonable legislators) were acting.

In endorsing some consideration of mental-state intentions, I do not mean to suggest that every appropriate use of legislative history must connect to mental states. Indeed, if the issue is put between "mental states" or "convention," the right answer is that mental states matter but that conventions have developed that accord pieces of legislative history a weight that will vary somewhat from what the most precise account of mental states would indicate in the specific circumstances, or more generally. Judges may reasonably rely on such conventions about respective weight without worrying too much how well they fit the circumstances of each statutory provision.

On both the mental state and conventional accounts, legislative history suggests how language is to be understood; pieces of legislative history are used to draw inferences about the subjective intentions of legislatures or the objective (i.e., fictional) intent of the legislature. Many of the arguments against a mental-states use of legislative history *also* apply against a conventional use. For example, the arguments that inquiry into legislative history complicates the task of judges and invites reliance on thin data, and that the use of legislative history involves improper delegation, apply against a conventional account, as well as a mental-states account.

IV. Legislative Reliance Over Time

There is a very powerful counterargument in favor of using legislative history to establish intentions of some kind. For nearly a century the courts have relied on legislative history, and for half a century such use was routine. Congress has legislated with that background. It has fairly relied on the courts giving significance to what have been said to be authoritative items of legislative history.[238] If the courts now depart from their previous interpretive practice, the product of Congress will be judged by standards it had no reason to expect. Even if a slow movement away from legislative history would be desirable, changing the standards of interpretation for laws that were enacted when legislative history was given great weight would be unfair.

238. *See, e.g.*, 134 CONG. REC. S2747–2748, S2760 (March 22, 1988) (statements of Sen. Hatch). Judge Wald has written that, if courts disregard legislative history because of worries about how it is produced, they "second-guess Congress's chosen form of organization and delegation of authority, and ... doubt its ability to oversee its own constitutional functions effectively." Patricia M. Wald, "The Sizzling Sleeper: The Use of Legislative History in Construing Statutes in the 1988–89 Term of the United States Supreme Court," 39 AM. U. L. REV. 277, 306–07 (1990).

V. Conclusion

The role of legislative history in statutory interpretation is now highly controversial in the United
States. Judges have good reasons to be very cautious about using that history. It should rarely
carry the day against language that is clear in
application. Even when language is unclear, judges
should not rely heavily on small bits of legislative
history that shed little light on specific intent or
purpose. Too many opinions read as if legislative
history is a decisive aid when any fair appraisal
indicates it should not be—either because the items
of history that judges cite only weakly support their
position *or* because pieces that are just as strong
support the competing position.[239] Judges should be
realistic and honest about legislative history, but
that is not a reason to abandon its use. No doubt,
judges manipulate legislative history in favor of
results they wish to reach, but they do the same
with language and other techniques of interpretation. For cases in which the impact of the language
is seriously in dispute, use of legislative history is
unlikely to render results that are more arbitrary
and unpredictable, and it can be valuable.

Various arguments against using legislative history have some force. It is subject to some manipu-

239. The overstatement of support is, of course, not limited
to legislative history. Judicial opinions are partly advocacy, and
judges typically overstate the strength of arguments that bolster
their positions.

lation in its creation by legislators, staff members, and lobbyists. Judges may misevaluate it, especially if the performance of lawyers in a case is very uneven. The search for relevant legislative history complicates a lawyer's task and generates expense for clients. Were courts to eschew the use of legislative history, it is possible, though by no means certain, that statutory drafting would become more careful. Use of most pieces of legislative history may compromise to a degree ideals of bicameralism and presentment to the chief executive. But none of these arguments is powerful enough to justify courts in abandoning all use of legislative history to determine the understandings of legislators. One very strong argument in favor of judicial reliance on legislative history is that Congress and state legislators have adopted many statutes on the assumption that legislative history would help guide interpretation.

Courts appropriately draw from legislative history for reasons other than determining mental states of legislators, but these uses should be regarded as supplementary, rather than alternative. Conventions undoubtedly have considerable importance in determining the weight of various pieces of legislative history, but these conventions rest largely on plausible general connections between various items of history and mental-state intentions.

CHAPTER XIII

CANONS OF INTERPRETATION

This chapter responds to Question 11 about judicial use of canons as interpretive guides for construing language whose application is difficult.[240] In the following chapter, I move from traditional canons of interpretation to some broad suggestions about interpretive approaches.

Judges often rely upon general canons of interpretation. These include techniques for understanding the meaning of language in context and traditional legal policies that cover all of statutory law or particular subjects.[241] William Eskridge divides canons into "precepts of grammar, syntax, and logical inference (the textual canons); rules of deference to the interpretations others have placed on the statutory language (the extrinsic source canons); and policy rules and presumptions (the substantive canons)."[242] I reserve discussion of rules of deference

240. "How far should interpretations of statutes be influenced by general canons of meaning and interpretation?"

241. At one time, the techniques for understanding language were called "maxims," the policy-oriented guides "canons"; but I follow more modern usage and refer to them all as canons here.

242. Eskridge, *supra* note 84, at 276. David Shapiro, in "Continuity and Change in Statutory Interpretation," 67 N.Y.U. L. Rev. 921, 925 (1992), expresses reservations about such a division, because "there is more to unify than to divide the

for Chapter Fifteen, because they involve a response to post-enactment events.

I. Textual Canons

Insofar as the textual canons are genuine guides toward understanding communications made by legislatures, their use corresponds well with an emphasis on textual meaning, and should be uncontroversial.[243] Here are three of these canons, rendered in English, with hoary Latin labels familiar to lawyers.

"The meaning of a word may be ascertained by reference to the meaning of words associated with it." *(Noscitur a sociis.)*

"When words of a particular or specific meaning are followed by general words, the general words are construed to apply only to persons or conditions of the same general kind as those specifically mentioned." *(Ejusdem generis.)*

"The expression of one thing is the exclusion of another." *(Expressio unius est exclusio alterius.)*

Suppose that a statute forbids transporting a woman for "prostitution or debauchery, or for any other immoral purpose." According to the second of these canons, the law definitely does not cover driving with one's wife from New York to New

canons that are likely to make a difference in statutory interpretation."

243. Dickerson, *supra* note 14, at 228, talks of "probabilities generated by normal usage or legislative behavior."

Jersey in order to inflict unjustified criticism on her parents. In this context, "any other immoral purpose" definitely does not mean every immoral purpose of which one can conceive.

The canon about understanding general terms in light of specific ones follows conventions of ordinary language, but it may do something more. It may alert legislators to the way statutory language will be understood, and may help them draft effectively. It may also have the consequence of favoring continuity over change.[244]

The objections to various canons about textual language run along three related lines: The canons are no help, they do not reflect ordinary use of language, and they conflict with each other. These objections, on examination, prove to be overstated or to misconceive the proper role of the canons. The answer to each objection is that the textual canons can be of limited assistance in context; one should not expect more.

Max Radin ridiculed the basis for the rule that the expression of one thing is the exclusion of another, which, he said, "is in direct contradiction to the habits of speech of most persons. To say that all men are mortal does not mean that all women are not, or that all other animals are not."[245] Radin continued, "It must be clear that the only value which such a maxim or axiom or rule could have would lie in the existence of an infallible or approxi-

244. *See* Shapiro, *supra* note 242, at 925, 929–31.

245. Radin, *supra* note 108, at 873.

mately infallible test of its applicability.... The question will accordingly be in every case, not whether or not the expression of one thing excludes everything else, but whether we are to deny or affirm this rule in this particular case ... for some other reason than its axiomatic force. ...."[246]

Radin is undoubtedly right that the inclusion of one thing is not necessarily the exclusion of another. However, the canon is more accurate for most directive language, including most legal language, than it is for his example. A statute that says, "Cats born after December 31, 1996, must be vaccinated" means by implication that cats born before that date need not be vaccinated.[247] Does it follow that this and other canons, failing to provide a nearly infallible test, are useless? What these canons do is to highlight features of much use of language, drawing the attention of judges to possibilities they should consider. Geoffrey Miller shows that a number of ancient legal systems have similar canons, and he explains how they relate to theories about implications in ordinary speech.[248] Hart and Sacks suggested that the canons indicate what is a linguistically permissible or more probable reading, not

246. *Id.* at 874.

247. *See* Geoffrey Miller, "Pragmatics and the Maxims of Interpretation," 1990 Wisc L. Rev. 1179, 1196; David Shapiro, *supra* note 242, at 928.

248. *See* Miller, *supra* note 247. The particular philosophy of language on which he draws is that of Paul Grice, the foundation of much work in pragmatics in linguistics. Pragmatics concerns the use of language in social context. *See also* M. B. W. Sinclair, "Law and Language: The Role of Pragmatics in Statutory Interpretation," 46 U. Pitt L. Rev. 373 (1985).

what is required.[249] Judicial opinions are rightly criticized when they make the textual canons appear to dictate results in some simplistic way, but it does not follow that the canons provide no help whatsoever.

In a famous law review article and subsequent book, Karl Llewellyn lined up competing canons, suggested that courts had available contradictory canons, and claimed that their choice of which canon to adopt was dictated by other considerations.[250] Against the maxim that the meaning of a word must be ascertained by reference to the meaning of words associated with it, Llewellyn offered, "A word may have a character of its own not to be submerged by its association."[251] So long as one does not take the canons as infallible rules, but as aids in context, one can see that these two "rules" are not incompatible with each other.[252] For particular statutory language, a judge would look to see if

249. Hart and Sacks, *supra* note 57, at 1191–92.

250. Llewellyn, "Remarks on the Theory of Appellate Decision and the Rules or Canons About How Statutes Are To Be Construed," 3 VAND L. REV. 395, 401–06 (1950); Llewellyn, *The Common Law Tradition: Deciding Appeals* (1960).

251. *The Common Law Tradition, supra* note 250, at 529.

252. Justice Scalia has remarked that Llewellyn's opposites mostly "merely show that the [first canon] is not absolute." Scalia, *supra* note 4, at 27. Shapiro, *supra* note 242, at 950, notes that many of Llewellyn's "parries" are "nothing more than a warning not to overdo it [i.e., application of the original canon]." Cass Sunstein has remarked that Llewellyn's claims of indeterminacy and mutual contradiction are greatly overstated. "Interpreting Statutes in the Regulatory State," 103 HARV L. REV. 405, 452–54 (1989).

a general word draws its character from the words around it, perhaps entertaining an initial assumption that it does so. If, however, the context signals that the general word has some independent meaning, a judge would give it that meaning. The "contradictory" canons could appropriately guide the judge's inquiry along these lines. Even were canons more directly contradictory than these are, they still might be able to help guide inquiries in context.[253] As Justice Scalia writes, canons may yield to contrary indications, but "that does not render the entire enterprise a fraud—not, at least, unless the judge wishes to make it so."[254]

II. Substantive Canons

Other canons reflect policies of the law. I have mentioned earlier the fundamental principle that

253. Dickerson, *supra* note 14, at 228, writes, "[A] given presumption or possibility is conditioned by the facts underlying its fellow presumptions and possibilities. This tends to make each situation unique and the particular reader is obliged to do a delicate, complicated balancing act."

254. Scalia, *supra* note 4, at 29. Macey and Miller suggest that, even if a canon gives strong guidance, judges freely decide whether or not to use particular canons in individual cases; thus, the potential applicability of a canon will not determine an outcome. "Canons of Statutory Construction and Judicial Preferences," 45 Vand L. Rev. 647, 648 (1992). I am assuming that, were a canon to have force in context about what language should mean, the canon should bear on the way judges interpret the language, even if they do not mention the canon in the opinion and they construe the language in a way different from what the canon indicates.

people should not be punished unless criminal statutes have given them fair warning that their behavior was illegal. This principle of fair notice applies to the criminal law, but analogous rules of clear statement are used for serious civil penalties such as forfeiture. Like many other legal policies, this principle of lenity connects to life outside of law; it reflects a pervasive sense that people usually should not be disciplined unless they have done something that they have definitely been told they should not do.

A long familiar canon of statutory construction has been the principle that statutes that change the common law should be strictly construed. This approach made evident sense when statutes created occasional ruptures in the fabric of the common law, but that canon has receded in significance and been widely criticized as our law has become increasingly statutory. David Shapiro suggests that the canon is analogous to another that disfavors implied repeals of statutes, and he defends both as reflecting the desirability of preserving continuity of law in otherwise close cases.[255]

Another traditional canon states that remedial statutes should be liberally construed. Since new laws are often remedial *and* change the common law, judges have had a kind of choice whether to adopt a "strict" or "liberal" construction. When the statute requiring automatic couplers was interpreted, the Court of Appeals emphasized its change in the common law and its penal force (fines for rail-

255. Shapiro, *supra* note 242, at 936–37, 941–50.

roads not in compliance);[256] the Supreme Court responded that the statute was primarily remedial in protecting the lives and bodies of workers.[257]

The canons suffered some eclipse as bases for interpretation when courts emphasized legislative history and legislative intent, but they have enjoyed a renaissance under the Rehnquist court, with its attention to text. In one sense, substantive canons are in tension with a "reasonable reader" approach to meaning, as well as a "legislator intent" approach.[258] If the natural reading of a statutory text points in the same direction as a substantive canon, the canon seems superfluous (though it could bolster the natural reading against a result suggested by some other criterion of interpretation). The canon mainly has bite when its application would yield a reading that is different from the reading that one would initially be inclined to give. Thus, the rule of lenity matters when judges might otherwise take a criminal statute as prohibiting behavior, but they hesitate because the statutory language may not forbid the behavior clearly enough. Scalia writes, "To the honest textualist, all of these preferential rules and presumptions are a lot of trouble. It is

256. Johnson v. Southern Pac. Co., 177 Fed. 462, 467 (8th Cir. 1902).

257. Johnson v. Southern Pac. Co., 196 U.S. 1, 17 (1904). Shapiro, *supra* note 242, at 938, suggests that the "remedial" canon has been mainly used when statutes do not impair existing arrangements of rights and liabilities.

258. However, if the "reasonable reader" is taken to be a lawyer familiar with practices of statutory interpretation, the reader may "bring" relevant canons to his understanding of the text.

hard enough to provide a uniform, objective answer to the question whether a statute, on balance, more reasonably means one thing than another. But it is virtually impossible to expect uniformity and objectivity when there is added, on one or the other side of the balance, a thumb of indeterminate weight."[259]

The substantive canons could fit comfortably with other guides to interpretation if they became a set of "off the rack" principles for statutory interpretation, known and relied upon by members of Congress.[260] Thus, for example, the Supreme Court has announced a canon presuming against extraterritorial application of United States statutes.[261] If legislators are aware of this canon, if they assume that the canon will be applied stably over time, they know that if they do not say anything, a statute will (probably) be interpreted to have only domestic application. If they want extraterritorial application, they will need to be explicit. A stable regime of canons could conceivably simplify both drafting and interpretation. But there are serious problems.

The canons are not stable over time, and legislators and their staff members, even if they are aware of relevant canons, can never be sure when a canon

259. Scalia, *supra* note 4, at 28.

260. *See* Daniel Farber, *supra* note 20, at 313 (1989); Eskridge, *supra* note 84, at *276–78.* Cass Sunstein, *supra* note 252, at 453–54, comments that any parallel with gap-filling terms for contractual interpretation is less than perfect because contract law is dominated by principles favoring autonomy and the market.

261. EEOC v. Arabian Am. Oil Co., 499 U.S. 244 (1991).

will be disregarded or outweighed by other considerations.[262] Perhaps Justice Scalia overstates matters when he says "these artificial rules increase the unpredictability, if not the arbitrariness of judicial decision";[263] but few observers believe that the canons, as they have been employed, much simplify the legislative task and increase overall predictability of statutory interpretation.

If the substantive canons are to be justified, it is in a more straightforward way: When statutory language is uncertain in its application, interpretation should accord with fundamental values of the legal system. The canons reflect such values, especially that of continuity.[264] So understood, canons are properly part of the mix in interpretation. These aids to interpretation are less central to decisions than some opinions suggest, but they often have a role. Canons should not be rigid barriers to interpretation, but when they are used as guides to consideration and as tie-breakers, they figure appropriately.[265]

As ideas of justice and policies of the legal system shift, room exists, as Cass Sunstein and William Eskridge have suggested,[266] for the decline of some

262. *See generally*, Eskridge, *supra* note 84, at 276–83.

263. Scalia, *supra* note 4, at 28.

264. *See* Shapiro, *supra* note 242.

265. *Id.* at 956–59, preferring guidelines as tie-breakers to guidelines as presumptions, and criticizing "super strong" clear-statement rules.

266. Sunstein, *supra* note 252, at 405, 462–63; Eskridge, *supra* note 84, at 148–51.

canons and the ascendance of others; but a canon needs to have more support than merely a scholar's or judge's idea of how things should be. Novel proposals about principles of interpretation do not become canons until they become rooted in judicial acceptance.

III. Conclusion

This chapter has defended modest reliance on both textual and substantive canons of interpretation. Many textual canons do reflect common use of language, and they are not nearly as opposed to one another as has sometimes been claimed. They are aids to understanding in context, not rigid rules. The substantive canons reflect significant legal policies. Such canons might give legislators considerable guidance about how to achieve objectives, but reliance on canons is too uneven to provide much assurance about the way particular language will be interpreted if its apparent meaning is unclear.

*

CHAPTER XIV

PROPOSED BROAD PRINCIPLES
OF INTERPRETATION

This chapter takes up Question 12,[267] which reaches beyond canons as they have traditionally been understood to other broad approaches to interpretation that have been suggested.

I. Some Proposed Interpretive Principles

When judges and scholars propose various principles of interpretation, exactly how these may relate to accepted canons can be complicated. Not all interpretive principles are considered canons, although the distinction between what counts as a canon and what does not is by no means sharp. A principle might fail to be a canon because it is not currently accepted or because it is at a level of generality more abstract than one would expect of canons that are to be applied in particular cases.[268] Some principles serve in large part to justify inter-

267. "How far should interpretations be influenced by principles and policies that bear on the law generally or on particular legal subjects?"

268. My suggestion that interpretation should accord with fundamental values of the legal system is an illustration of such an abstract principle.

pretive approaches that are already widespread. These principles may provide a solid foundation for various existing canons and may guide the way those canons are understood; the principles may also be a basis to generate new, related canons. Other principles may connect less closely to existing canons; their reflection of important values may be urged as a basis for developing new canons, or as a kind of substitute for canon-based approaches.[269] Thus, Cass Sunstein claims that a special task of the judicial branch is the protection of poorly represented minorities; this principle could underlie a new canon that legislation that significantly affects minorities should be interpreted in a manner favorable to members of the minorities.[270]

Existing canons have a hold on judges that derives partly from dominant practice. Principles that explain those canons make a similar claim. The further that proposed principles depart from present judicial practice, the more their force must rest on their appeal to desirable political and moral principles. Even if a judge is persuaded that a principle of interpretation might be desirable, she will understandably be hesitant to depart sharply from a dominant contrary practice.

I shall examine a number of proposed principles of interpretation. Since I am focusing neither on the

269. In a widely cited article, *supra* note 252, Cass Sunstein is taken as proposing a set of novel canons, yet one section heading is "A Concluding Note: The Post–Canonical Universe." *Id.* at 502.

270. *Id.* at 472–73.

parameters of the term "canon" nor on whether sitting judges should immediately adopt novel principles, I do not discuss which principles should be regarded as canons or exactly how far various principles may stray from existing practice.

I. The Relevance of Constitutional Standards

One principle that is widely accepted *in some form* is that judges should construe statutes in accordance with constitutional standards. Thus, if a statute can be comfortably construed in a way that favors free speech or in a way that might constitute a constitutional violation of free speech, it should be construed to favor free speech. When a litigant plausibly asserts that one statutory reading would be unconstitutional, and a court can avoid determining exact constitutional limits by interpreting the statute differently, it has a reason to do so.

Serious questions arise when the approach of favoring free speech is followed in two other contexts: Should a court favor free speech values when it concludes that an interpretation either way would be constitutional? Should a court indulge even a strained reading of statutory language in order to avoid declaring a far more natural reading a violation of the First Amendment, or in order to avoid resolving that issue?

About decisions to favor free speech when interpretations counter to free speech would survive constitutional challenge, the following argument might be made. "The Constitution sets limits on legislatures, but beyond those limits legislatures have authority to decide what to do for the general welfare. As long as it acts within the boundaries set, a legislature has as much right to steer close to constitutional limits as to stay far away.[271] The Constitution has no preference for free speech apart from the speech it actually protects." [272]

This position is not nonsensical, but it is mistaken. The Constitution reflects basic values, as well as exact limits, values such as racial and religious equality and freedom of expression. Acknowledging that interpretation is properly responsive to fundamental values of the legal system, courts should recognize the Constitution as one repository of those values, affecting interpretation even within the range where legislatures have a choice. Further, if the legislature is to infringe on those values, it should make a definite, clear decision to do so, and

271. In a subtle form, this argument would need to take account of possible limits the Constitution sets on legislative action that are not judicially enforceable. *See* Sunstein, *supra* note 252, at 468–69. For example, the constitution may implicitly restrict various legislative motivations that judges are not equipped to investigate. Conceivably, statutory interpretation might reinforce such a restriction. I do not discuss this nuance here.

272. Frederick Schauer, in "Ashwander Revisited," 1995 SUP CT REV. 71, is critical of the judicial practice of avoiding constitutional questions and argues that it is not justified as a way of showing respect for the legislature. *See also* Richard Posner, *The Federal Courts* 85 (1985); Richard A. Posner, "Statutory Interpretation—In the Classroom and in the Courtroom," 50 U. CHI L. REV. 800, 816 (1983).

should not have indefinite statutory wording interpreted to that effect. Constitutional values properly figure even when it is clear that actual unconstitutionality is not at issue.[273]

The issue of strained interpretation is more troublesome. The Supreme Court has said on occasion that it will interpret statutes to avoid constitutional issues, and to that end it has sometimes given statutory language a very unnatural interpretation.[274] If members of a court know they would decide that either interpretation would be constitutionally permissible, their rejection of the otherwise natural interpretation merely because it "raises a constitutional issue" unfairly circumscribes the power of Congress. Suppose judges recognize that the most natural reading, by far, raises a constitutional issue, but the judges believe the reading is definitely constitutionally permissible. That is the reading they should adopt.

The harder circumstances are when judges are not sure how they would decide a constitutional issue or, though having a definite view that the natural reading is unconstitutional, they deem it prudent to avoid finally resolving the constitutional issue on that occasion. If judges have actually decided that they would hold a measure unconstitutional if interpreted one way, their different interpretation

273. *See* Sunstein, *supra* note 252, at 462–63; Eskridge, *supra* note 84, at 148–51–74.

274. United States v. Seeger, 380 U.S. 163, 174–183 (1965); Welsh v. United States, 398 U.S. 333, 342–43 (1970). *See also* United States v. Rumely, 345 U.S. 41, 47 (1953).

is, in practical effect, a kind of constitutional decision. But the decision lacks authority as a constitutional holding. Exactly when courts should avoid resolving constitutional issues is well beyond the scope of this book. But I assume that avoidance is sometimes proper, and that a strained reading of debatable statutory language may be an acceptable price.

II.   Reasonable Legislators?

Writers have suggested principles of interpretation that build from assumptions about legislative pursuit of statutory objectives. In a well-known passage, Hart and Sacks proposed, "The statute ought always to be presumed to be the work of reasonable men pursuing reasonable purposes reasonably, unless the contrary is made to appear."[275] On occasion, this recommendation has been challenged as reflecting a naive picture of the legislative process, one that fails to recognize that many measures can be explained only by the pursuit of narrow objectives and compromises. But it is clear that Hart and Sacks were mainly making a normative recommendation whose wisdom does not necessarily depend on how well it reflects what actually motivates legislators.[276] The normative argument goes something like this: Whatever bases legislators have

275.   Hart and Sacks, *supra* note 57, at 1124–25. *See also id.* at 1378.

276.   *See* Sunstein, *supra* note 252, at 435.

for making statutes, the law will develop most smoothly and constructively if judges interpret language whose application is debatable as designed to promote reasonable public purposes. So understood, the proposal raises important and controversial questions about the proper relationship between courts and legislatures.

In the face of the lessons of public-choice theory and various critical attacks on objective motions of public rationality, Hart and Sacks may seem to undermine the process value of compromise and to arrogate too much power to courts, allowing judges to interpret in light of reasonable purposes as they happen to see them. If legislatures are to have priority in democratic governance, perhaps judges should be less creative in construing legislative purposes.

Textualism is one response. When judges stick faithfully to the meaning of words as an ordinary reader would understand them, they have less opportunity to write their own proclivities into legislation. One of the leading textualists, Frank Easterbrook, has suggested more particular techniques of interpretation that would prevent courts attributing to legislatures their own ideas about desirable policy.[277] If legislation authorizes courts to develop flexible statutory terms in light of changing values, the courts should do so. In that event, judges should openly appraise values as they would in common law decision making; they should not attribute their choices to the enacting legislature. According to

277. Easterbrook, *supra* note 66, at 533.

Easterbrook, "[U]nless the statute plainly hands courts the power to create and revise a form of common law, the domain of the statute should be restricted to cases anticipated by its framers and expressly resolved in the legislative process."[278] This approach, Easterbrook claims, faithfully reflects the nature of legislative compromises, prevents legislators from extending their power beyond their terms, takes a realistic view of judicial abilities, and adopts a liberal view of the relation of public and private spheres by not expanding the public sphere unless that has been clearly directed.[279]

If legislatures sat like small committees with a limited range of responsibilities, able to repair gaps in the statutory fabric quickly and with little cost, Easterbrook's proposal would have much to recommend it. Why should judges, rather than new legislators, decide what directions to pursue in unforeseen instances? If members of a city council were imagining only horse-drawn carriages, let judges stick with those until the council decides it wants to include automobiles. Unfortunately, Easterbrook's proposal founders on the realities of the legislative process.[280] Legislators have massive responsibilities

278. *Id.* at 544. In limiting a statute to cases anticipated and expressly resolved, Easterbrook would afford some provisions less coverage than a natural reading of the text by a reasonable reader would indicate.

279. *Id.* at 547–51.

280. That is, it founders unless one is willing to sacrifice a lot in legal coherence in order to curb judicial power and keep as many matters as possible out of the public sphere. I should note

and a tremendous range of potential subjects of legislation. Typical legislatures are ill equipped to respond to every new situation not conceived by original legislators. Demanding that legislators respond in this way would put a great strain on the legislative process.

Richard Posner's proposal that judges try imaginatively to reconstruct what the enacting legislative would have wanted[281] shares with Hart and Sacks the idea that judges should try to make sense of legislation and to build a coherent approach to novel situations. The approach shares with Easterbrook the belief that judges should be faithful to legislative compromises, not attributing to legislation some unrealistic reasonable purpose.[282] As Posner himself has recognized, when statutory terms result from secret compromises, it may be very hard to reconstruct what the legislators would have wanted, but he nonetheless has asserted, "A document can manifest a single purpose even though those who drafted and approved it had a variety of private motives and expectations."[283]

When courts can sensibly reconstruct what an enacting Congress would have wanted *and* when that interpretation fits the language comfortably,

that, were Easterbrook's overall method followed for legislation that repeals earlier statutes and withdraws matters back from the public to private spheres, the result would be less recapture for the private sphere than if judges adopted a more active method of interpretation.

281. *See* Posner, *supra* note 125.

282. *Id.* at 192.

283. *Id.* at 196.

Posner's approach promises more fruitful relations between legislatures and courts than does Easterbrook's. Two aspects of Posner's approach are much more debatable. Suppose that judges believe the necessary reconstructive efforts would require a highly strained reading of the textual language, as in the LSD penalty case I discussed in Chapter Nine.[284] I agree with Posner that even then an attempt to make sense of a statute is preferable to assigning specific language its ordinary meaning,[285] but the contrary, now dominant position, that judges should not stray so far from ordinary textual meaning is also defensible.

The second aspect of Posner's approach that is seriously debatable is what judges should do when reconstructing what the enacting Congress would

284. United States v. Marshall, 908 F.2d 1312 (7th Cir. 1990) (en banc), *aff'd sub nom*; Chapman v. United States, 111 S.Ct. 1919 (1991).

285. T. Alexander Aleinikoff and Theodore Shaw, "The Costs of Incoherence: A Comment on Plain–Meaning, *West Va. Univ. Hosp., Inc. v. Casey*, and Due Process of Statutory Interpretation," 45 VAND L. REV 687, 689 (1992), argue that courts should "ensure that the meaning imposed upon a statutory text bears, at a minimum, a plausible connection to some practical purpose that makes sense in our legal system." The authors criticize an opinion for the Court by Justice Scalia rejecting recovery for expert witness fees in civil rights cases on the ground that there is no plausible basis for a distinction between civil rights plaintiffs and other litigants who receive such fees. What the authors propose is a reasonable minimum requirement, unless the text is unambiguously clear to the contrary. It is interesting, however, that, when Congress subsequently overturned the legal rule established in *West Va. Univ. Hosp.*, it adopted a categorization as to who could recover that was narrower than that suggested by Aleinikoff and Shaw.

have wanted is difficult, as it often will be. Very roughly, the possibilities are to adhere to the ordinary meaning of the text, to reconstruct as best one can, to adopt the Hart and Sacks approach of ascribing reasonable public purposes to the legislators, or to develop the law in the way judges deem most sensible. In favor of the last approach, one may argue that reconstruction á la Posner is often impossible and that efforts to follow the Hart and Sacks approach lead judges to impute their own purposes in any event. The wisdom of the last approach depends substantially on appraisals of post-enactment events, a subject for subsequent chapters.[286]

Jonathan Macey has developed a powerful argument in favor of the basic proposal of Hart and Sacks as an antidote to self-interested legislation.[287] He acknowledges that much legislation favors narrow interests rather than public good, but regards this as unfortunate. Legislators would prefer to conceal their adoption of such provisions, not to make their selling out to private interests obvious. If judges interpret ambiguous provisions as if they were designed to serve public purposes, that will produce better substantive results than if judges carry out the hidden purposes of legislators acting to serve private interests. It will also force legislators to be explicit if they aim to promote private

286. Various difficulties with imaginative reconstruction have led Posner to support an approach that is more simply "pragmatic." *See* Richard Posner, *The Problems of Jurisprudence* 73 (1990).

287. Macey, *supra* note 165.

interest at public expense, and will thus reduce the amount of legislation of that sort. Drawing upon a Madisonian concern about factions, Macey concludes that interpretive techniques to impede interest groups fit with our constitutional design. Courts should, therefore, take at face value statements about public objectives, and not seek to dig out hidden benefits for private-interest groups.

Einer Elhauge points out that we have no clear standards as to what is in the public interest, and that we therefore lack any clear line between public-serving laws and those serving private-interest groups.[288] To take an example that is close to home for university students and their families, do various forms of governmental financial support for higher education mainly serve the public objective of education, or do they mainly subsidize middle class citizens whose advanced education will greatly increase their future earnings? Other groups that benefit from various statutes may have less appealing arguments that their subsidies advance public welfare, but probably nearly all can tell some story along those lines. Despite these difficulties, I believe that judges can often distinguish between provisions that mainly serve public interests and those that redistribute wealth in a way few people would try to defend openly. In any event, if judges give weight to stated legislative purposes, and rely on particular canons of interpretation that reflect tra-

---

288. Elhauge, *supra* note 219, at 49–59. *But see* Eskridge and Frickey, *supra* note 164, at 55–56 (focusing on the suspicious combination of concentrated benefits and distributed costs).

ditional ideas of sound legislation, they can accomplish much of what Macey recommends without themselves determining that any particular legislative aim lies outside of what would serve the public.

III. Conclusion

This chapter has examined some proposed interpretive principles that are broader than canons. Some of these are reflective of dominant practice; others involve elements of reform. The idea that judges should interpret statutes in accordance with constitutional standards is widely accepted. I have suggested that constitutional values have some pull, even when actual unconstitutionality is not at issue. Judges should not give a text an unnatural reading if the natural reading is definitely constitutional; but strained reading may sometimes be warranted in order to avoid declaring the natural reading unconstitutional. Hart and Sacks's famous proposal, that statutes ought to be regarded as the work of people pursuing reasonable purposes reasonably, does not depend on its descriptive accuracy. It may be defended as inhibiting legislation that serves private interests at the cost of the public welfare. On the other hand, it may be challenged as unfaithful to legislative compromises and as conferring too much authority on courts. Judges and critics reasonably disagree about just which attitude judges should take toward legislative provisions whose coverage is uncertain in context.

The substantive canons as well as proposed principles of interpretation that may justify existing canons or lay the basis for new ones raise profound questions about the degree to which courts should do anything more than attempt loyally to implement whatever it is that legislators may have tried to do. I have suggested that the courts are not simply agents who try to carry out the wishes of a superior legislature, that they have some independent role in protecting the subjects of legislation and in making judgments about fairness and sound policy. That conclusion itself is not highly controversial, but what is disputed is the degree to which courts should be creative in developing a rational, sensible law. I favor a somewhat more creative role than may be currently accepted as the dominant paradigm, if one can speak of such a thing; but there is room for a range of reasonable positions along a spectrum. Thus far, I have discussed these problems as they bear on construing original meaning, and have not distinguished between those judges deciding soon after enactment and those construing a statute decades later. But the issues raised by post-enactment events press questions about a proper judicial role even more insistently.

CHAPTER XV

THE SIGNIFICANCE OF POST-ENACTMENT EVENTS: CLARIFICATIONS

The next five chapters tackle the most fundamental issue about statutory interpretation: Should interpreters regard a statutory enactment as fixed in time, not giving weight to events after passage, or should they take statutory language as an evolving part of the whole body of the law, considering various post-enactment events as affecting how the language should be understood? Here is how one of the strongest proponents of "dynamic" interpretation has put it. "A court should not interpret a statute against its apparent textual or legislative history meaning unless circumstances have changed to undermine original legislative assumptions, the legislature has sent inconsistent directives, or new meta-policies justify a different interpretation."[289] This approach gives substantial weight to text and legislative history, but it also allows their combined force to be outweighed on many occasions. Which post-enactment events, if any, should be able to

289. William N. Eskridge, *supra* note 86, at 333 (1989). *See also* T. Alexander Aleinikoff, "Updating Statutory Interpretation," 87 MICH. L. REV. 20 (1988), defending a "nautical" approach to interpretation in which the courts (the captains in the nautical analogy) make many specific choices.

override or alter original meaning? Why should any be able to do so? One critical aspect of these basic questions is the relation between courts and administrative agencies.

I. Open-Ended Terms

I begin with three clarifications. On occasion, legislatures adopt open-ended terms that invite flexible application in light of changing conditions. A direction that a public utility may charge a "fair rate" is an obvious example; what constitutes a fair rate changes with economic conditions, such as inflation and the expected return on investment for a utility company. A prohibition on "restraints of trade," such as the Sherman Act provides,[290] leaves courts to develop on a case-by-case basis just which restrictions on full competition are illegal. No one doubts that post-enactment events affect the proper application of such broad terms, although it is often debatable whether a particular statutory term is of this variety. The meaning of the statutory term can remain constant while applications shift.

II. Facts That Reveal a Conflict of Purpose and Specific Intent

Another kind of post-enactment event is the recognition of facts that reveal a conflict between a statute's underlying purpose and the specific intent

290.   15 U.S.C. § 1 (Supp. V 1993).

for a provision. I suggested such a scenario in connection with whether employers may give voluntary preferences to blacks under Title VII of the Civil Rights Act of 1964.[291] Let us assume that a farseeing person could have realized at the time of enactment that forbidding voluntary affirmative action would severely inhibit enforcement against straightforward discrimination that blacks suffer. Let us also assume that relevant considerations indicate that broad purpose here should win out over conflicting specific intent.[292] Actual enforcement efforts reveal a conflict that only very perceptive people would have foreseen when the statute was enacted; but, in retrospect, one could say that ideal judges, acting immediately after the statute was adopted, would have recognized the conflict and permitted voluntary affirmative action. Most judges would not then have been sufficiently insightful to reach this result, but current judges should not disregard truths that were perceivable at adoption and that post-enactment evidence has made clearer and more widely understood.

291. One way of thinking about Title VII is as having two purposes: (1) increasing employment opportunities for groups such as blacks and women; and (2) eliminating racial and gender classifications—with time revealing that fulfillment of the two purposes was in opposition with respect to preferential affirmative action. *See* Eskridge, *supra* note 84, at 30–32.

292. I remind the reader that I am using this problem as an illustration, that disagreement with my perspectives about this case or affirmative action more generally does not undermine the force of the illustration. Of course, if a reader thinks purposes should never win out over specific intentions, he or she will conclude that this kind of increased understanding of a conflict between the two is irrelevant.

In what follows, I pay little attention to situations in which statutory terms evidently invite changing applications or in which post-enactment events demonstrate facts that could have been grasped by very perceptive persons at the time of enactment. I focus on whether post-enactment events can actually alter what would be the best interpretation of a statutory provision.

III.   The Limits of General Hermeneutic Theories

My third clarification is of a different sort. Statutory interpretation is related to other forms of textual interpretation, and it might appear at first glance that some general theory of interpretation, some hermeneutic theory, can tell us whether post-enactment events should figure in interpretation. According to one persuasive and influential hermeneutic theory, that of Hans–Georg Gadamer, interpretation of earlier texts is inevitably against a horizon of current perspectives and concerns.[293] On the central point that modern interpreters bring their own background and perspectives to bear, Gadamer is broadly representative. One might move from this presupposition to a conclusion that originalism in any form is proved wrong by hermeneutic theory; but the move would be unwarranted.

293.   Gadamer, *Truth and Method* 304–06 (Joel Weinsteimer and Donald G. Marshall trans., 2d ed. 1989). *See generally* Eskridge, *supra* note 84, at 4–5, 64–71, 346–51; Georgia Warnke, "Law, Hermeneutics, and Public Debate," 9 YALE J.L. & HUMAN. 395 (1997).

If we think of fields as diverse as history, anthropology, literary criticism, and the performing arts, we can recognize that one possible form of interpretation is to replicate as closely as one can some original understanding. One will never succeed perfectly—hermeneutic theory tells us that much—but it still may be appropriate to try, that is, to elucidate an original conception as well as one can, rather than to focus explicitly on more modern understanding.[294]

Whether focusing on original understanding, to the exclusion of post-enactment events, is a desirable strategy of interpretation must be assessed in terms of the values of a legal system and the best relations between legislatures and courts. The difficulty of the task of discerning original understanding as time lapses, the inevitable coloring of modern perspectives that any evaluation of that sort involves, may well be reasons to envision a different role for courts. But the inexorable barriers to perfect understanding do not themselves constitute a decisive argument against trying. In many forms of moral and political evaluation, we rightly ask people to do what they are capable of doing only imperfectly, e.g., assessing arguments without personal bias, acting with disinterested care. Even if "original reader understanding" or "original intent" is re-

294. *See* Kent Greenawalt, "Interpretation and Judgment," 9 YALE J.L. & HUMAN. 415 (1997) (responding to Warnke, *supra* note 293). Professor Warnke indicates that she did not mean to reject this possibility. Georgia Warnke, "Reply to Greenawalt," 9 YALE J.L. & HUMAN 437, 437–438 (1997).

garded as an interpretive construction rather than an elusive fact to be discovered, it is possible that interpretation in this mode will be more fruitful than any other. General hermeneutic theory cannot establish that originalism is a misguided approach to statutory interpretation.

General hermeneutic theory cannot itself resolve the debate between originalists and evolutionists. In the final analysis, an approach that rests on original understanding above all else can only be rejected on the basis of political and moral reasons rather than some overarching hermeneutical theory. The next four chapters address those kinds of reasons. Chapter Sixteen concentrates on administrative interpretation, briefly discussing the settled practice of courts following statutory decisions rendered by prior courts. Subsequent chapters consider other post-enactment events that may influence interpretation.

IV. Conclusion

In addressing whether judges should understand statutes as evolving, I am not focusing on provisions that are designed to convey authority to courts to develop law over time. I am also not focusing on situations when new facts more sharply reveal conflicts of specific intention and purpose that a wise judge could have perceived at enactment. General hermeneutic theories can illuminate aspects of interpretation, including legal interpretation, but they cannot resolve the way judges should interpret statutes.

CHAPTER XVI

ADMINISTRATIVE INTERPRETATIONS

One frequent issue that is crucial to the separation of powers is the scope courts should give to interpretations of statutes by independent administrative agencies and the executive branch. Question 13 poses that issue.[295] Let us suppose that a statute is adopted in 1999. An independent agency or executive department responsible for directly administering the statute renders an interpretation in 2000 and applies the statute accordingly. The particular issue does not come before a court until 2006. Might judges properly adhere to the agency interpretation, even if they conclude that had they been deciding a similar case prior to the agency interpretation, they would, or might, have preferred the competing interpretation? If agency interpretations are to be given this kind of independent weight,[296] on some

295. "In considering whether events after a statute's adoption should matter, how should courts regard the interpretive responsibilities of administrative agencies and executive departments?"

296. If the only deference that a court gives to an agency opinion is a kind of respectful consideration, such as an appellate court might give to the opinion of the trial court on some issue of law, that does not amount to independent weight. Were that the only influence of the agency opinion, a court would not conclude that it might have reached the opposite result had it otherwise been very well advised but lacking the agency view.

233

occasions courts will be led to conclusions different from those they might have reached had the agency not interpreted as it did. Various grounds might justify judges giving such weight to administrative interpretations.

I. Original Intent

___

An agency or executive decision on an issue might constitute strong evidence of original intent. When legislation concerns an administrative arm of the government, agency officials commonly make detailed recommendations and work with members of the legislative branch in subsequent drafting. Further, those in the agency are subject to legislative control if they diverge in some serious way from actions legislators want and expect. An agency decision shortly after a law is adopted may reflect prior understandings both about the import of specific language and about overall purposes. Judges can infer from the decision something about what members of the legislative branch thought, and they can even more confidently infer what administrative officials believed at enactment.[297]

The strength of these inferences will, of course, vary from case to case. If the administrative decision is quasi-judicial and made by people who are largely independent of others in the agency, little

297. The inferences about administrators will be directly relevant if judges conclude that the intentions of those in the government who draft statutes count, even though they are not in the legislative branch.

can be inferred about the mental-state intentions of those who worked on the statute. The further that final statutory language departs from what agency representatives proposed, the less an agency decision may reflect what legislators intended. Still, on many occasions, agency decisions after the fact are evidence of mental-state intentions leading to enactment. If this evidentiary value is the main significance of agency decisions for courts, agency officials should probably be explicit about the degree to which their judgments are based on original understanding.

If a judge adopts an approach to statutory interpretation that excludes mental-state intentions, this version of an original-intent reason to defer to agency decision disappears, but perhaps some closely analogous reason could survive. Could one take an agency decision as evidence of the way a reasonable reader would have understood language? The plausibility of this possibility depends on two factors: how much the reasonable reader is allowed to know about the background of legislation, and the lapse in time between administrative determination and judicial interpretation. The better informed the reasonable reader is assumed to be, the more an agency decision might be evidence of the way he would have understood statutory language. The greater the time between agency decision and judicial inquiry, the more likely it is that a judge might think the agency had a more accurate sense of how a reasonable reader would have understood a text, upon enactment, than would judges deciding years later.

If judges use agency decisions to draw inferences about original intent (or a reader's original understanding), that represents only a limited compromise with the basic idea that statutory meaning is fixed at enactment. We are supposing that even a farseeing outsider could not predict what the agency would decide, and that the agency decision tips the balance of evidence about original intent enough to affect the court's construal of a provision. Assuming that meaning is ideally determined in part by an accurate appraisal of mental-state intentions, the force of the agency decision provides important evidence about those intentions; the decision does not alter the meaning of the language. However, because the agency decision creates previously unavailable evidence, it may influence which judicial assessment of meaning is soundest, in light of all the evidence available to a court.[298] Thus, taking a subsequent agency decision as important evidence of original intent is consonant with the idea that only pre-enactment events determine meaning; but it does not fully accord with a notion that the best judicial appraisal of meaning remains constant after enactment.

298. That is, the best possible judicial assessment of meaning right after enactment (given then-available evidence) may be different from the best assessment after the agency decision. This shift in best assessment differs from my assumption about the relevance of Title VII enforcement efforts in showing a conflict between purpose and specific intent. As to that, I assumed that a farseeing person could have recognized the inevitable conflict even before actual enforcement began.

II. Expert Advice

Another way in which an agency or executive decision might be regarded is as expert advice about the way a legal provision should be understood. The value of such "advice" will depend partly on how objective the procedure for agency decision is—are the commissioners attempting to reach a balanced decision, taking everything into account, or are they in some sense partisans of one side or the other?[299] Officials of ordinary executive departments usually have more partisan responsibilities than those in independent agencies.[300] More commonly than in executive departments, independent agencies use formal procedures that ensure fuller presentation of competing positions than do standard processes of executive decision.

The idea of "expert advice" is that a court will defer to the agency's expertness, taking its view as correct, unless the view strikes the court as clearly wrong. It is as if I ask my doctor for advice, and he provides it, with an explanation. On the basis of the information I receive from him, I do not see why his recommended course of action is as desirable as an alternative he rejects; but I conclude that, because

299. Judge Learned Hand wrote an insightful opinion in which he suggested that courts might assign different weight to different kinds of decisions of executive agencies. Fishgold v. Sullivan Drydock & Repair Corp., 154 F.2d 785, 789–90 (2d Cir.), *aff'd*, 328 U.S. 275 (1946).

300. One thinks, however, of claims of independent agency "capture" by industries that are regulated.

he understands a lot more than I do, I will act according to his processing of the information rather than my own. If I consult five doctors and get the same advice from each of them, my inclination to do what they say will be even stronger. We can imagine a court taking a similar view in response to an agency decision about the meaning of a statute within the agency's domain. As with the advice of doctors, the force of advice will be much stronger if all the commissioners agree than if they are divided three-to-two about approaches.

As I have described the "expert advice" approach, it may seem close to the idea of the court's giving respectful consideration, but not independent weight, to the agency decision. The distinction I mean to draw can be illustrated by the difference between my understanding my doctor's explanation, so that I believe on my own judgment that his recommended course of treatment is best, and my not understanding why that course is best, but accepting the doctor's judgment. I have assumed that a court giving "respectful consideration" finally decides on the basis of its own full understanding of the substantive merits of competing claims. The court deferring to expert advice may reach a decision different from that which its own full understanding of the substantive merits yields, on the ground that the agency probably knows best.

This "expert advice" approach moves slightly farther away from rigorous adherence to the concept that meaning is fixed at enactment than does use of agency decision as evidence of original intent. It shares with the "original intent" approach both the notion that the ideal sense of meaning does not alter after enactment, and the notion that the best assessment of meaning by a court may shift—in this instance, because the court now possesses previously unavailable expert advice. Use as "expert advice" differs, however, from use as evidence of intent in the following way: The expert advice, we are assuming, does not actually persuade the court by the force of its reasoning. This gives the post-enactment event of the agency decision somewhat more independent significance than it has if all it is taken to do is to stand as evidence of an original intent that has always existed.

III. Expectations

As time passes after an agency decision, expectations develop on the basis of agency regulation that accords with the agency's decision about what a provision means.[301] Because courts have some reason not to upset settled expectations, they should follow the agency decision if the matter is otherwise close. On this rationale, the court may actually believe that, on balance, the agency determination

301. The length of time between agency decision and judicial interpretation is not as crucial for the "evidence of original intent" and "expert advice" approaches. Under either, the force of agency decision is about as great if it comes shortly before a court's actions rather than years earlier. Of course, if the significance of original intent declines over time, the significance of evidence of original intent will decline as one input for a court's interpretation.

was wrong when rendered and would be wrong now, were it not that the agency had decided the way it did some years ago.[302]

Courts afford this kind of deference to earlier judicial precedents in common law systems. The system of precedent involves not only common law and constitutional cases but also interpretations of statutes.[303] Indeed, courts often say that the strength of *stare decisis* is heightened in statutory cases, as compared with common law and constitutional ones, because the legislature can alter interpretations of which it disapproves and its silence indicates acquiescence.[304] The first court decides a statutory issue one way. The second court follows the interpretation even though it believes it may be wrong. From the point of view of the second court, the action of the first court has effectively altered how a provision should be understood.[305]

302. In most instances, a court does not reach the conclusion that the agency decision *was* wrong. The court needs to decide only that it should follow the agency whether or not the agency decision was correct (or desirable). The court need not decide whether the agency decision would have come out better the other way.

303. For an unusual case suggesting otherwise, see Windust v. Depart. of Labor and Indus., 52 Wash. 2d 33, 38, 323 P.2d 241, 244 (1958).

304. *See* Lawrence C. Marshall, " 'Let Congress Do It': The Case for an Absolute Rule of Statutory Stare Decisis," 88 MICH L. REV. 177, 184–85 (1989). As his article's title indicates, Marshall supports an absolute rule, not because of congressional acquiescence, but because this approach will constitute the best allocation of responsibilities.

305. A notable example was the U.S. Supreme Court's adherence to an earlier ruling that professional baseball is not subject

On the understanding I am suggesting here, a court regards an agency decision in a manner similar to its own prior precedents. Though it may be more willing to reject agency views than its own prior decisions, the court follows an agency determination unless that seems plainly wrong. The reason is the expectations the agency has created. Giving agency decisions this kind of weight obviously sacrifices the idea of meaning being fixed at enactment. The best judicial interpretation is now understood as being affected by the ways in which other people have understood the statute since enactment. Once this concession is made, the way is open to argue that other evidence about settled expectations should affect interpretation. Such expectations can arise from compatible understandings of private parties, although they are most likely to be created by authoritative administrative decisions.

Insofar as respect for expectations represents a breach in the notion of meaning fixed at the time of enactment, it is eminently sensible. If settled expectations matter, and expectations have been settled, that should affect the way a provision is understood. Statutory precedents already make this an aspect of our system of statutory interpretation. Given respect for precedent, no judges are pure "originalists," guided only by their best sense of

to the antitrust laws. *See* Toolson v. New York Yankees, Inc., 346 U.S. 356, 357 (1953); Flood v. Kuhn, 407 U.S. 258, 282–285 (1972). Peter Strauss argues that the common law nature of our legal system, in which respect for precedent is a crucial aspect, points strongly toward an evolutionary reading of statutes. Strauss, *supra* note 34.

original meaning. The reasons that support respect for precedent also support some respect for administrative decisions.

IV.   Partners in Lawmaking

Yet another rationale for courts following agency decisions is that agencies are partners of the courts in the interpretation of statutory provisions that relate to their activities. This rationale is close to the "expert advice" approach, but it differs in two important respects. First, the focus is on allocation of function and shared responsibility, rather than on comparative expertness (although, of course, if agencies are expert, that is a reason to conceive of them as having a function of legal interpretation). If legislatures with the responsibility to make law have chosen to confer a degree of that responsibility on agencies, courts should respect the political legitimacy of the administrative decisions that follow. Second, a court accepting an agency as a partner may follow the agency decision even if it believes it was probably mistaken or undesirable.[306] A court relying on "expert advice" concludes that an agency decision was probably right, although the court may not fully understand the reasons that moved the

306. If the court assumes that the interpretation of some terms properly depends on policy judgments by an agency, "undesirable" is a more apt term than "mistaken" for a view that the agency did not decide as it best would have. *See* Chevron U.S.A. v. Natural Resources Defense Council, Inc. 467 U.S. 837, 845, 866 (1984).

agency. In just this respect, the partners approach moves yet further from the theory that meaning is fixed at enactment. Here, as under the expectations approach, the post-enactment event decisively alters the way a provision should be understood.

We may compare this approach with an alternative model under which the agency is subordinate to the courts in legal interpretation. This is the model that appellate courts follow with trial courts. Appellate judges listen to what the trial judges say about the law, but they decide on the basis of what they think is the best interpretation.[307] Why should administrative agencies not be treated as subordinate in the same manner as trial courts, able to make crucial factual determinations and resolve many mixed questions of law and fact, but rendering decisions about law subject to complete judicial review? No evidently correct answer to the choice between these two alternatives about the way courts should interpret statutes directed at administrative agencies falls into place, once one understands the separation of powers.

It is helpful here to be more precise about the kinds of decisions agencies make. A great many statutes broadly delegate to executive agencies (including here independent administrative agencies, such as the Federal Communications Commission, and arms of the executive branch, such as the

307. That is, they do not say, "We might decide one way about what the law means, but since the trial court has decided the other way, we will go along with it." In this respect, decisions about law are different from certain discretionary choices that are left to trial judges.

Internal Revenue Service) the authority to make more precise rules. Under this authority, agencies make policy determinations, such as whether cars should be required to have seat belts, and they issue rules that directly regulate private behavior. Agencies make four different kinds of decisions that courts may review. They (1) interpret the legal standards of the authorizing statutes; (2) make explicit policy judgments on which their own regulations and decisions are also based; (3) interpret the regulations they themselves have created; and (4) make quasi-adjudicative factual assessments that largely determine whether an individual instance falls within the regulations.

As to each of these functions, the question arises of how strict judicial review of an agency determination should be. During the Vietnam War, for example, it became crucial what kind of evidence was required to support factual determinations that someone who claimed conscientious objection to military service was insincere.[308] No one doubts that agencies, not courts, should be making explicit policy judgments within the domains of agency responsibility, but over the decades the courts have become increasingly demanding about the conditions under which those decisions are made and the justifications that agencies provide for them.[309]

308. I describe briefly the way review changed from being highly deferential to highly undeferential, in "All or Nothing at All: The Defeat of Selective Conscientious Objection," 1971 SUP CT. REV. 31, 44–46.

309. *See, e.g.*, Stephen Breyer, "Judicial Review of Questions of Law and Policy," 38 ADMIN L. REV 363, 383; Peter H. Schuck

The interpretations of the content of statutory provisions and of the content of agencies' regulations involve more traditionally "legal" decisions. In recent years, the courts have given a high degree of deference to agency interpretations of their own regulations, on the assumption that agency competence is especially relevant when an agency interprets legal standards it has created.[310] John Manning has pointed out that this practice creates a serious possibility of abuse; an agency may be able to evade strict requirements for the way it creates regulations by issuing an unclear rule and then interpreting it in the way it wants.[311] The decision on which I am concentrating in this chapter is the other form of agency interpretation—interpretation of the authorizing statute itself. Should what the agency determines about that carry independent weight with a reviewing court?

The U.S. Supreme Court's present approach is highly deferential to agency interpretations made during rule-making or adjudication procedures,

& E. Donald Elliot, "To the Chevron Station: An Empirical Study of Federal Administrative Law," 1990 Duke L. J. 984, 1057–1059 (showing markedly increased overall judicial deference to agency decision making after *Chevron*). *But see* Linda Cohen and Matthew Spitzer, "Solving the Chevron Puzzle," 57 LAW & CONTEMP PROBS. 65, 103 (1984) (finding a subsequent decline in judicial affirmations of agency decisions in the period following that analyzed in the Schuck–Elliot study).

310. Kenneth C. Davis & Richard J. Pierce, Jr., *Administrative Law Treatise* § 6.10 at 282 (3d ed. 1994).

311. John Manning, "Constitutional Structure and Judicial Deference to Agency Interpretations of Agency Rules," 96 COLUM. L. REV 612, 683–84 (1996).

once the court determines that the statutory provision is not itself clear. In the leading case of Chevron U.S.A. v. Natural Resources Defense Council, Inc.,[312] the term needing to be interpreted was "major stationary sources" in the Clean Air Act of 1977. The question was whether the Environmental Protection Agency had appropriately adopted a plant-wide definition of "stationary source" (thus allowing an increase of pollution from one emitting device if there was a corresponding decrease from another device). Although the term "stationary source" sounds like a technical one, not inviting flexible rulemaking by the agency, the Court decided that, in the absence of a specific congressional intention about the applicability of the term, courts should accept the agency construction if it "is a reasonable policy choice for the agency to make." The Court regarded as perfectly appropriate the agency shift in the construal of "stationary source" that accompanied a new administration with new environmental policies. Both in its equation of this legal interpretation with a "policy choice" and in its standard of reasonableness, the Court's approach is very deferential to agency judgment.[313] Is that degree of deference warranted?

312.   467 U.S. 837 (1984).

313.   Thomas Merrill has written of *Chevron* ("Judicial Deference to Executive Precedent," 101 YALE L.J. 969, 969–70 (1992)): "Indeed, read for all it is worth, the decision would make administrative actors the primary interpreters of federal statutes and relegate courts to the largely inert role of enforcing unambiguous statutory terms."

It is critical the degree to which the statutory provisions that govern agency action are intertwined with a legislative conferral of law-making responsibility on agencies and with a special competence of the agency that derives from its members' expertness and the greater time they can devote to issues that concern the agency.[314] Three other relevant factors are accountability, processes of agency decision, and methods of judicial review. When the interpretation of unclear statutes depends substantially on judgments of policy, one might think these judgments should be made by agencies that have greater political accountability than do courts.

Courts appropriately yield much more authority to agencies when they resolve issues in formal rule-making or quasi-judicial determinations than when officials construe statutes in their ordinary executive functions (as when a high police official instructs officers about the way to apply a statute regulating confessions). Judges should defer only after agencies have considered competing claims in a fair, reflective, and balanced way.

The structure of judicial review is also very important. Does one court, or many, review the deci-

---

314. For suggestions that *Chevron* deference is too great, see Breyer, *supra* note 309, at 372–73 (1986); Sunstein, *supra* note 252, at 444–46. Because *Chevron* drastically altered the standard for review of agency decisions, it cannot be justified as carrying out the design of Congress for statutes enacted prior to the decision. Congress legislated against the background of the prior standards. *See* Manning, *supra* note 311, at 623–25. For Manning, the decision rests mainly on considerations of accountability that are of constitutional derivation. *Id.* at 625–27.

sions of a particular agency? If review is by many courts, each one will be less expert than a single court could be, and variant interpretations will increase the chances for disruptive uncertainty about the law. These consequences will be substantially avoided if all courts are instructed to follow most agency interpretations. Peter Strauss has argued powerfully that a primary justification for the *Chevron* doctrine lies in the limited number of cases the Supreme Court takes.[315] Most administrative cases will be decided finally by other federal courts. If different courts offer different interpretations, the law will be much less clear and stable than if the single agency interpretation is usually respected.

One must take a sensitive overall view of the legal system in order to decide how far agencies should be viewed as partners in lawmaking. There are strong reasons to accord them a substantial role in this regard—to conclude, as did Hart and Sacks, that "An interpretation by an administrative agency charged with first-line responsibility for the authoritative application of the statute should be accepted by the court as conclusive, if it is consistent with the purpose properly to be attributed to the statute, and if it has been arrived at with regard to the factors which should be taken into account in elaborating it."[316]

315. Peter L. Strauss, "One Hundred Fifty Cases Per Year: Some Implications of the Supreme Court's Limited Judicial Resources for Judicial Review of Agency Action," 87 COLUM 1093, 1095, 1118–22 (1987).

316. Hart and Sacks, *supra* note 57 at 1380.

V. Conclusion

What effect should judges give to interpretations of statutes made by independent administrative agencies and executive departments? Should they sometimes accept those interpretations without deciding that they would have made the same decisions in the absence of the agency rulings? The major grounds for judicial deference to agency interpretations are that they (1) provide evidence of original intent; (2) constitute a form of expert advice; (3) create expectations that should be fulfilled; and (4) represent decisions by politically responsible partners in lawmaking. The last two rationales move furthest from the notion that meaning is fixed permanently at enactment.

*

CHAPTER XVII

CHANGES IN THE CORPUS OF LAW AND EXTERNAL CONDITIONS

Many things may change between enactment and interpretation, other than judicial and executive interpretations that are directly relevant to the issue a court must resolve. In this chapter, addressing Question 14,[317] I examine the relevance of a number of these.

I. Changes in the Corpus of Law

To what extent should interpretation take account of changes in the entire body of the law from the time a statute is adopted? No subsequent statute repeals a provision, but new statutes, or changes in constitutional law or common law, make a particular interpretation of a provision fit better with the law overall than it would have at the time of enactment. For this discussion, I shall assume that the textual language of a provision would best have been understood one way at enactment, but that the initial best reading of the text now fits

317. "How should courts treat changes in the corpus of law and other post-enactment events that might alter the way statutory language could best be interpreted?"

more awkwardly with the law as a whole than would a plausible alternative reading. Should this make a difference? If it does make a difference, what was once the best reading may no longer be so.

This unsettling question of the relation of statutory directives to other law touches the heart of legislative authority and process. The simplest approach is that legislatures have authority to enact provisions; if a subsequent legislature wants to change what a provision does, it must repeal or alter that provision. This simple approach is too simple.

Congress is not able subtly to adjust the entire body of statutory law each time it enacts a new statute. Legislation takes time and effort; the process is cumbersome. No staff member reviews every statutory provision to see which adjustments would make them all accord best with the new dispensation. No one proposes changes in the language of a wide range of related provisions to accomplish that accord. One cannot expect Congress to bring the entire body of statutory law in line with its present perspectives and newest laws. Congress must pick and choose what it does; and leave the rest. If any institution is to smooth out the rough edges, to treat statutory law, and law as a whole, as some kind of coherent structure, it must be the courts.

Some reference to the existing body of law is uncontroversial. Here is what Justice Scalia, a strong textualist originalist, wrote for the U.S. Supreme Court in 1991,[318]

> Where a statutory term presented to us for the first time is ambiguous, we construe it to contain that permissible meaning which fits most logically and comfortably into the body of both previously and subsequently enacted law.... We do so not because that precise accommodative meaning is what the lawmakers must have had in mind (how could an earlier Congress know what a later Congress would enact?), but because it is our role to make sense rather than nonsense out of the *corpus juris*. But where, as here, the meaning of the term prevents such accommodation, it is not our function to eliminate clearly expressed inconsistency of policy and to treat alike subjects that different Congresses have chosen to treat differently.

As this quote intimates, serious disagreement is not over whether *some* reference to subsequent law is relevant, it is over whether subsequent law should carry weight only when a provision's original meaning is highly debatable or should also affect interpretation even of a provision whose initial sense was apparently more straightforward. Another, related, point of disagreement is how much importance present legal coherence[319] should have

318. West Va. Univ. Hosp., Inc. v. Casey, 499 U.S. 83, 100–01 (1991). Bradley Karkkainen, *supra* note 4, at 408, sums up Justice Scalia's view: "A judicial interpretation of a statute must be faithful to the text, but the meaning of the text itself can change over time as the legal landscape changes."

319. I use the term "present legal coherence" because one might, under either a "reasonable reader" or "legislative intent"

in comparison with other criteria of interpretation. Finally, people may disagree about how far afield judges should go. Should they consider only matters that connect fairly directly to the disputed provision, or should they conceive of the law as entire law, for example, treating deregulation of one industry as evincing a deregulatory philosophy that affects interpretation of provisions regulating other industries?

Between the passage of Title VII in 1964 and the first time the U.S. Supreme Court had to decide if it allowed voluntary affirmative action, two significant legal changes had taken place.[320] First, the Court had decided in Griggs v. Duke Power Co.[321] that employers can discriminate unlawfully without intending to, if they use employment tests or other standards for hiring with a disproportionate racial impact, and the standards are not required by "business necessity." Second, the executive branch had undertaken stringent compliance procedures for companies contracting with the federal government. The combined effect of these measures was to put many employers in a serious bind if they could not undertake "voluntary" racial preferences in hiring and training programs. If they did not reach out to hire minorities, they might be found to have

approach, or some combination of the two, refer to coherence with the law that existed at enactment. Justice Scalia, *supra* note 4, at 17, has written, "We look for a sort of 'objectified intent'— the intent that a reasonable person would gather from the text of a law, placed alongside the remainder of the corpus juris."

320.   Daniel A. Farber, *supra* note 260, at 316–17.

321.   401 U.S. 424 (1971).

discriminated against them; if they did reach out, they risked discriminating against whites. These changes properly could affect how the crucial provisions of Title VII were understood in their relevance for affirmative action.

No one has emphasized coherence in the law more than Ronald Dworkin. Courts, he says, should look at Congress as a single entity over time, interpreting one statute in light of what else Congress has done.[322] This idea of a single coherent body of statutory law has appeal, but its vision of legislative authority is troubling. Dworkin qualifies his focus on coherence with a notion of "fairness" that judges should be sensitive to public opinion,[323] but the difficult implications of coherence are clearest if we focus on that alone.

These implications are revealed by sharp changes in the political climate, of the kind that have occurred with some frequency in Great Britain,[324] and

322. Dworkin, *supra* note 6, at 338, writes, "Integrity requires [the ideal judge] to construct, for each statute he is asked to enforce, some justification that fits and flows through that statute and is, if possible, consistent with other legislation in force." In this formulation, other statutory law is emphasized to the exclusion of common law and constitutional law. Under Dworkin's entire theory, all other law is relevant, but it is not clear whether related statutory law is more important than related common law.

323. *Id.* at 340–41.

324. The two major parties in Britain have often had a significant ideological division. With the leaders of the executive branch also serving as members of Parliament, and with legislators voting loyally for party programs, changes in legislative and executive power occur together, and changes in government have

occurred in the United States from 1930 to 1933, by which time the Democrats had taken over Congress and the Presidency from the Republicans under dire economic conditions. To make the analysis clear, I will assume that left-leaning, welfare-state Democrats take over the national government from right-wing, laissez-faire Republicans, and that judges use coherence as the crucial standard of interpretation when a text is unclear.

The Democrats enact their first statute, and it quickly arrives at a court for interpretation. Since the vast majority of the statutory corpus of law is now laissez-faire, on doubtful issues this new law will be interpreted to harmonize with it, not to be more welfare-oriented than the language strictly requires. At this stage, judges will continue to interpret the older laws in a laissez-faire vein, since the single welfare-state law has made an imperceptible dent in the whole corpus of law.[325] The judges are aware that the present Congress *will pass* more welfare-state laws, but treating existing statutory law as a single fabric, they interpret doubtful provisions in a laissez-faire way. As Congress passes more laws, interpretations shift. The more welfare-state laws Congress passes, the more welfare-state

sometimes resulted in great shifts in legislation. The ability of Parliament to change direction for the country has also been affected by Britain's having a unitary, rather than federal, system.

325. I put aside the reality that, if the Republicans have been in power for more than a decade, most judges, Republican appointees, will decide in a laissez-faire way anyway; we are talking about what judges *should* do according to this theory, not what they *will* do.

oriented will be judicial interpretations of laws that it and earlier Congresses previously adopted.

If one grants that interpretation should shift with time, heavy focus on the existing corpus of law does not seem apt for radical political developments. When a new Congress adopts a law that is the first in a program of welfare-state measures, judges believe with near certainty that many such other measures will soon follow. In these circumstances, a court should concentrate overwhelmingly on the aims of the new law, and not worry too much about fit with the rest of the then-existing corpus of statutory law.[326] If a court takes this view, its interpretation of the first welfare-state law will not become progressively more welfare-statist as Congress proceeds to adopt similar laws.

Assuming that statutory interpretation should be somewhat responsive to strong political changes,[327] emphasis on the coherence of statutory law makes too much depend on the amount of legislation the new Congress has managed to get enacted. Courts, rather, should be somewhat responsive in statutory interpretation to the programs and attitudes of that Congress.

I have argued against too much emphasis on the coherence-of-statutory-law view for statutes that reflect radical political change; but a great many

326. For similar reasons, a statute that makes a self-conscious and sharp break with existing common law should not be interpreted to make the minimal breach with common law principles.

327. *See* Eskridge, *supra* note 86, at 343 (1989).

statutes have nothing to do with radical change. Courts may see that successive Congresses have treated related subjects and perceive no difference in basic outlooks that motivated their treatments. In that event, judges should try to harmonize effects when the language of a provision may easily be interpreted in more than one way. As a consequence, the best interpretation of an earlier statute may change as that statute is followed by related provisions.

This conclusion helps answer the problem of whether the discernible attitudes of a present Congress toward past interpretations of legislation should matter. Courts have sometimes relied on Congressional silence in the face of an interpretation as showing acquiescence in the interpretation.[328] But inaction can be the product of so many different causes, a court is rarely justified in concluding that a Congress has effectively endorsed an interpretation simply because it has done nothing. Even re-enactment of the provision and the rejection of alternative proposals may be unsure signs of a positive attitude toward what the court has done.[329] On some occasions, however, material in subsequent legislative history may give a strong signal about the way members of Congress regard judicial interpretations. In the instances when a court is justified in making the judgment that Con-

328.   *See generally* Eskridge, *supra* note 84, at 241–242.

329.   For a case bearing on whether conscientious objectors were eligible for citizenship that involved rejected proposals in Congress as well as re-enactment, see Girouard v. United States, 328 U.S. 61, 69–70 (1946).

gress does approve an interpretation, that is *one* reason to stick with the original interpretation.[330]

II. Issues of Congressional Authority

I now turn briefly to deeper questions raised by judicial focus on the corpus of law or present political attitudes, whether the emphasis is on coherence with the existing body of law, apparent legislative endorsement, or highly likely programs of legislation. Any focus on later law or Congressional attitudes may seem to take away from the authority of the enacting Congress and give too much power to a new Congress. According to some authors, each Congress should be limited in its power to what it enacts, not effectively altering the meaning of laws it does not touch by adopting related measures.[331] But should laws that no longer reflect the mood of the country continue to be interpreted in the old

330. One might take the attitudes of the present Congress as evidence of the views of a former Congress, but, especially as time elapses, "the views of a subsequent Congress form a hazardous basis for inferring the intent of an earlier one." *See* Waterman Steamship Corp. v. United States, 381 U.S. 252, 269 (1965). It is more accurate to suppose that the attitudes of the present Congress matter for their own sakes. *See* Brudney, *supra* note 227, arguing that the reason for courts to pay attention to these signals is that their rejection "imposes significant opportunity costs on Congress." *Id.* at 7. As William Eskridge has pointed out, *supra* note 84, at 152, judges can more confidently assess the attitudes of crucial members of Congress if there is close monitoring of the courts' statutory decisions by members of Congress or their staffs.

331. *See, e.g.,* Easterbrook, *supra* note 66, at 548–49.

mode just because the new Congress cannot get around to changing everything?[332] The idea that interpretation should continue to be in light of the visions of those who enacted the law gives each Congress the maximum power over what it actually enacts and the minimum power to alter interpretation of what it does not enact.[333] The view that interpretations should be influenced by the outlook of the current Congress gives each Congress the maximum power to alter law while it remains in office, at the price of having its power decrease quickly after it leaves office, as its own laws are affected by the views of subsequent Congresses.

When one assesses these alternatives against broad questions of political philosophy, the view that interpretation should continue to accord with the visions of the enacting Congress is politically conservative. Because any Congress will be limited as to what it can do, faithful interpretation of old laws will impede political change. The alternative approach fits well with a perception that shifts in programs and outlooks are healthy, that new political winners should be bogged down to the minimum possible.

How is one to resolve this tension? No one doubts that our political system, with its separation of powers, dual legislative houses, federalism, guaran-

332. Hart and Sacks emphasized that legislatures do not have the time or the resources to continually monitor and amend stale statutory precedent, *supra* note 57, at 1359.

333. Of course, the power of the President and the Senate to put different judges on the bench will have a considerable effect, but, again, I am putting that aside.

teed rights, and its less than cohesive political parties, makes radical national political change very difficult. Judicial focus on the enactors' vision helps carry out this innate conservatism. But perhaps the basic structures of our system make political change so difficult that courts should lean toward interpretive techniques that moderate, rather than reinforce, the conservatism of these structures. Because I incline to the latter view, I favor readings of older statutes that "bring them up to date" when the language can reasonably be read either way. Giving great independent weight to the interpretations of administrative agencies has this effect, insofar as the agencies themselves are responsive to political change, and alter their understandings of statutory terms in light of the political climate and the objectives of the present government.[334] Courts should also give some weight to parallel statutory changes that reflect new objectives.

III. Other Altered Conditions

Should judges interpreting statutory provisions take into account changes, since enactment, in conditions outside the legal system? Of course, legal changes typically accompany nonlegal ones, but the question here is whether judges should restrict themselves to changes within the law or give independent weight to external changes. I have already

334. In Chevron, U.S.A., Inc. v. National Resources Defense Council, Inc., 467 U.S. 837, 857–58 (1984), the Supreme Court treated such responsiveness as appropriate.

discussed one change that is not strictly within the law, a shift in the political philosophy of those running the government. I turn now to broader social changes.

William Eskridge has suggested, "At the level of society and culture, changed circumstances include new understandings about individual, group, or institutional behavior; revised professional consensus or popular mores; and fresh factual information or intellectual paradigms."[335] I shall concentrate on changes in factual evaluation and moral understanding.

My "factual" example is built on "fair-trade" laws. As I discussed in Chapter Eight,[336] states during the 1930s passed laws that allowed manufacturers to agree with retailers that they would not sell below a set retail price; they further provided that even non-signing retailers were bound to sell at the price set with other retailers. The Miller–Tydings Act plainly authorized states to enforce actual agreements between manufacturers and retailers, but the crucial language was not clear about the status of the non-signer aspects of state laws. Most members of Congress (or at least those who had thought about it) meant to approve the non-signer clauses;[337] but the textual language itself points modestly against their endorsement. The case was

335. Eskridge *supra* note 84, at 53.

336. See text accompanying *supra* notes 140–42.

337. However, as I have mentioned, it is possible that legislators consciously chose to avoid explicit language that would make that anticompetitive objective obvious.

close, but a Supreme Court majority held that the state non-signer provisions were not validated.[338]

The case was decided in 1951, and opinions about the utility of fair-trade laws might have evolved from the time the law was enacted until then. Let us suppose that in 1951 the nearly unanimous view of economists was that fair-trade laws, and particularly the crucial non-signer provisions, were detrimental to the economy. The changed view was produced by an alteration in economic conditions and a more developed understanding about the economic effects of fair-trade laws.[339] My question is whether, in an otherwise close case, a court should consider a changed assessment of the effects of fair-trade laws. If so, then obviously the best interpretation of the meaning of a provision could evolve with social conditions and expert opinions in a discipline.

My "moral understanding" example builds on a famous (or, rather, infamous) construal of a statute that forbade transporting a woman across state lines for "prostitution or debauchery, or for any other immoral purpose."[340] The defendant had

338. Schwegmann Bros. v. Calvert Distillers Co., 341 U.S. 384 (1951). The majority had to overcome the common contrary construction of executive agencies and other courts. I here disregard that aspect of the case.

339. The fact that Congress did subsequently validate non-signer provisions, in the McGuire Act amendments to § 5(a) of the Federal Trade Commission Act, ch.745, 66 Stat. 631 (1952) (codified as amended at 15 U.S.C. §§ 45(a)(1–5) (1952)), probably shows that my assumptions are not accurate.

340. Caminetti v. United States, 242 U.S. 470 (1917) (interpreting the Mann Act).

crossed a state line with the purpose of cohabiting with his mistress. The Supreme Court said that this was an "other immoral purpose" and upheld a conviction. Many people think the decision is outrageous; they believe, more particularly, that traveling with one's lover across state lines is too dissimilar from prostitution and debauchery to be covered by such general language. Here, I want to assume that, when the statute was adopted, people of a more moralistic age thought that all sexual intercourse outside of marriage was very close to prostitution or debauchery and that the Court's actual construction of the statute would have seemed natural. However, by the time the Court decided the case, public mores had changed and people thought that crossing state lines with one's lover, if a wrong at all, was a wrong of a different magnitude and character than the two activities named in the statute. For them, the Court's reading would have been unnatural. Should the Court have taken such a shift in moral understanding into account?[341] If so, the best interpretation of a provision could shift accordingly.

A court's reliance on changed factual or moral understanding is much more controversial than reli-

341. I am assuming in this discussion that the Court should not have concluded that the statutory phrase actually invited a flexible reading according to developing moral sentiments. If one viewed the phrase in that way, it would follow that the Court should have been responsive to the change in moral attitudes. See Posner, *supra* note 125 at 194, suggesting that the Mann Act may have been adopted to back up state regulation of family and sex, and that regulation should change with changes in moral climate.

ance on agency decisions or changes in the surrounding corpus of law. But I think it is justified. Courts are expected to keep the common law up to date in light of changing factual and moral understandings, and in otherwise close cases it is appropriate for them to do this for legislative provisions. We must always keep in mind the reality that Congress cannot easily go back and rewrite all its statutes as social conditions and opinions change. When the language can be comfortably construed in that manner, and other standards of interpretation leave the issue nearly in equipoise, courts should render interpretations that are not too removed from present understanding about what is appropriate regulation.[342]

Some of the canons mentioned in Chapter Eleven have the effect of rendering changes in social understanding relevant. The idea that people should receive "fair warning" that their behavior is criminal provides a notable illustration. A term that once gave fair warning may cease to do so over time, particularly if no pattern of enforcement reminds people what the term covers.[343] Someone might contend that fair warning has to be judged at the

342. *But see* Farber, *supra* note 20, at 283, 307–09, suggesting that judges should not rely on changes in public opinion. Cass Sunstein has an interesting discussion focused on the statutory phrase "induce cancer," and how it should have been interpreted as increasingly minute risks became discernible with advancing technology. Sunstein, *supra* note 252, at 496–97. He believes that changing technology rendered the phrase ambiguous.

343. The *Caminetti* case involved a serious problem of lack of fair warning.

moment of enactment; but, as I have argued earlier, fairness should concern the adequacy of language for those who are actually prosecuted.[344] Fair warning, thus, should be gauged in relation to those people, not hypothetical persons who might have been prosecuted immediately after enactment. Thus, we see that this canon itself can render some social changes relevant, even if they are not reflected directly in the law in some way.

IV. Conclusion

In the United States at least, it is widely agreed that changes in the overall body of law can affect how an unclear statutory provision should be understood. To some degree, statutes should be fitted to the existing corpus of law. However, courts should also pay attention to radical political changes that have not yet had much impact on enacted law. People can reasonably disagree as to how far judges should be responsive to the perspectives of the legislatures that sit when the judges decide cases. My analysis here hardly scratches the surface, but I conclude that some responsiveness is appropriate.

I suggest that changes in factual and moral understandings that new law does not reflect heavily may also affect interpretation; and these changes may affect interpretation even when judges do not

344. It is possible that active prosecution and judicial interpretation would provide fair warning about the coverage of a phrase, years after enactment, even though the phrase did not give fair warning when first enacted.

conclude that the legislature has chosen phrases that invite judicial development over time.

*

CHAPTER XVIII

MORAL AND POLITICAL JUDGMENTS OF JUDGES

No one doubts that actual judges are influenced to some degree in legal decisions by their own moral and political opinions, but it is debated whether they should rely self-consciously on those opinions or try to be completely guided by other criteria of interpretation. This delicate subject reaches all areas of legal decision. Although it is more starkly posed in common law and constitutional adjudication, it also arises in statutory interpretation. Question 15[345] asks whether self-conscious judicial reliance on moral and political opinions is proper.

As I noted earlier, judges must implicitly make some moral and political judgments in order to develop principles of interpretation. The question here is whether they should adopt an approach that leads them to make such judgments in particular cases. Without doubt, legal interpretation sometimes requires moral and political judgments focused on particular cases; but a judge's philosophy of interpretation might be that she should refrain from relying on her own perspectives, rather drawing all moral and political judgments from the cor-

345. "Should judges rely self-consciously on their own moral and political judgments?"

pus of law, the purposes of legislators (for statutes and constitutions), and community morality. Because all these sources may be indecisive, and because anyone must make certain moral judgments in order to decide what constitutes community morality, judges cannot avoid relying on their own moral and political judgments on every occasion.[346] But, except when statutory terms invite judges to appraise issues from a moral perspective, judges should rarely rely explicitly on their own moral views in statutory cases. Since legislators are responsible for statutes, judges should rely mainly on the moral views of the enacting legislators and those whom they represent, with some attention to the views of present legislators and citizens.

Yet, I am hesitant to say that no scope whatsoever remains for the judges' own deliberate evaluations. Let us reconsider the *Weber* (affirmative action) case, and put aside the effective enforcement and changed-circumstances arguments I have made in previous chapters. Suppose that Justice A concludes in 1979 that the statutory language appears to forbid voluntary affirmative action in the form of preferences, and he determines from the legislative history that most members who actually considered the subject in 1964 probably intended that result. But Justice A also concludes that members of Congress were concentrating on forbidding outright racial discrimination against blacks and did not give much thought to preferences that would *help* blacks. Justice A regards the issue of voluntary

346. *See* Greenawalt, *supra* note 104, at 216–20.

affirmative action as very important. He is aware that the country is deeply divided about the issue, and he strongly doubts that members of the present Congress have the fortitude to make a clear resolution one way or the other.

If, on all these assumptions, Justice *A* believes that any racial categorization is deeply wrong, his giving the language of the antidiscrimination sections their apparent meaning makes sense. But suppose, instead, that Justice *A* is convinced that voluntary affirmative action is a critical means for eliminating the scourge of racism. I think he would appropriately vote to read the statute as not forbidding that means. If I am right, in unusual cases judges self-consciously may give some weight to their own moral and political judgments. (They do so, of course, not *because* these judgments are their own, but because they represent their views about which judgments are actually best.) In these cases, I believe it is a difficult question whether they should be candid about all their grounds for decision. Perhaps, judges should not engage, in written opinions, what really are the best answers to deeply controversial moral questions (except insofar as those answers happen to be intertwined with what are mainly legal arguments).

In summary, if statutory language calls on judges to make moral judgments, they appropriately rely partly on their own moral evaluations (as well as giving some weight to understandings of others in the community). Apart from these situations, explicit reliance on self-conscious moral evaluations should be minimal. In some rare circumstances, actual reliance may be appropriate, but it is doubtful whether that reliance should appear in written opinions.

Chapter XIX

How Should Courts Understand What They Do When They Take Account of Post-Enactment Events?

In the previous four chapters, we have seen the powerful arguments for courts interpreting statutory provisions somewhat differently than they might have, immediately upon enactment. There is room for substantial disagreement over exactly which post-enactment events should count and how much weight these events should be given in relation to other criteria of interpretation, but all judges and scholars are in accord that *some* post-enactment events matter to some degree. In this chapter, I consider the subject of Question 16: How should judges understand and explain what they are doing, when they use standards of interpretation that may yield development from the time of enactment in the way in which a provision is best applied.[347]

347. "If judges interpreting statutory language appropriately conceive of its desirable application as shifting over time, should they understand the meaning of a statute as changing, or should they regard some desirable present applications as deviating from the statutory meaning; and should they be candid about whatever their understanding is?"

Lying in the background is always a question of candor, which I shall face first. Perhaps courts should not acknowledge all the subtleties of interpretation. What exactly constitutes candor about "evolving law" is linked to a feature of most of the cases I have discussed. Typically, a court does not need to resolve what a correct interpretation would have been twenty years ago; it need only decide what is the best interpretation *now*. If judges explicitly use standards of interpretation that give weight to post-enactment events, honesty does not compel them to admit that the best interpretation would have differed twenty years earlier; honesty requires only their implicit acknowledgment that a present decision does not necessarily resolve what would earlier have been the best interpretation. Since judges do not have to say anything directly about earlier interpretation, the only failure of candor is for them to speak as if the proper interpretation has definitely remained the same through time. I assume that judges should be honest in the sense of not asserting (in opinions) claims that they recognize do not accord with the ways in which they actually decide cases. Thus, candid judges should not announce principles of interpretation that would fix meaning at enactment if they employ principles according to which meaning may develop over time.[348]

348. For a piece that recognizes some of the strongest arguments against full candor and provides powerful reasons for rejecting most of them, see David L. Shapiro, "In Defense of Judicial Candor," 100 HARV L. REV. 731 (1987).

How should judges understand what they are doing if they accept some version of evolving law? For some provisions, it may be plausible to conceive of a steady meaning, with the best interpretation of applications developing over time. One might think of "other immoral conduct" as "immoral conduct that seems closely similar to prostitution or debauchery." Traveling with one's lover for sexual purposes was (on my artificial assumption) once within that category; over time it fell out. One could say that the statutory meaning of "other immoral conduct" has remained the same, although applications have shifted. Whether the Miller–Tydings Act validates non-signer provisions cannot comfortably be handled in that way; either the language of the federal act includes them within its exemption, or it does not. If the best interpretation of the provision shifts in this respect, the provision's meaning changes. I shall simplify in what follows by assuming that changed meaning is at issue, and not merely changed applications of steady meaning.

Three different conceptualizations might explain why courts give a meaning to a provision that they would not justifiably have given it at enactment. One approach is to say that the best meaning has not changed, but modern judges rightly have deferred to someone else's judgment and accepted a meaning that may not be the best. The second approach is to say that statutory meaning, as best interpreted, has actually changed. The third approach is to say that statutory meaning does not change, but that courts have authority to deviate from statutory meaning for strong enough reasons.

The first approach works for some kinds of situations. Insofar as judges defer to judicial precedents and agency decisions, based on expectations and partnership in interpretation, they can adopt the first understanding. They can assume that the best interpretation of what statutory language "really" means remains constant, while accepting that, in a complicated process of government, judges often accept others' decisions about meaning without themselves resolving whether the interpretations by others really are best. In this respect, a court treats its own earlier decision or an agency interpretation as a trial judge treats an appellate decision it must follow. (However, a court may reject an agency interpretation or overrule its own previous decision; a trial court cannot reject a binding appellate decision.) The trial judge accepts an interpretation of her higher court without necessarily resolving whether she thinks the interpretation is mistaken. On this view, judges can give weight to *certain* post-enactment events without acknowledging that best interpretations of meaning really do change.

This approach does not work, however, for post-enactment events that are not themselves determinations of a provision's meaning. When judges take guidance from changes in the corpus of law, in the political philosophy of governments, and in factual and moral understandings within the culture, the issue of change in meaning cannot be circumvented by emphasis on deference. A judge who thinks clearly is then driven to the second or third approach.

The second approach is more straightforward. It acknowledges that the best interpretation of a provision's meaning may change. If statutory provisions are conceived, not as isolated fragments whose meaning must be fixed at enactment, but as standards formulated in language that continue in authority over time as aspects of an ongoing system of governance, their meaning may be understood as changing (to a degree) responsively to changes in various conditions.

We may think of the third approach as a way to avoid the second approach, or as a supplement to it. With trusts that individuals write, a judge, according to a doctrine of *cy-pres*, has the power to say that the terms cannot be carried out, or *should* not be carried out, in light of certain social changes. The court then establishes terms that are explicitly understood as different from the terms of the trust, but that carry out its general objectives. If shifts in desirable results under statutes were so viewed, judges would recognize that they properly reach different final legal conclusions as conditions change,[349] but they would say that they are altering statutory terms rather than correctly attributing a changed meaning to them.

Could one reasonably prefer this third approach to the second as a general account? Allowing judges to reject the terms of statutes gives them at least as

349. On the idea of statutory *cy-pres,* see Farber, *supra* note 260, at 309–14, 331; Eskridge, *supra* note 84, at 123.

much unchecked power as does allowing them to conceive that statutory meaning sometimes changes. Thus, the third approach, in principle, is hardly more innocuous about judicial authority than is the second. Those who oppose active judicial responses to changed conditions might favor the third approach just because its admission of judicial power is so stark that judges would be hesitant to proceed in a way that lays bare their exercise of the power to reject statutory terms.

I can imagine two more neutral theoretical reasons for adopting the third approach. One is that the meaning of all communications is fixed at the time of utterance, and that statutes are a form of utterance. The other is that the meaning of statutes is fixed at the time of enactment according to the right political theory about legislative authority. Whatever may be true for other utterances, the first assumption is evidently false for imperative language that plays a continuing role in the social life of a group of people. There is no reason to assume that its meaning must remain constant. As for the political-theory reason, much of this book has been devoted to rejecting its rigid political view of legislative authority. In short, we have no good basis for supposing that courts can supplant statutory meaning but that that meaning cannot actually change.

In some circumstances, however, the idea of court imposition of new terms may be the most accurate description. If judges rely on general purpose and changed conditions to reject a specific outcome that Congress plainly intended with fairly clear language in a narrow section, the most candid statement would be that the court is declining to apply that section according to its meaning.

To summarize this chapter, the best understanding of what occurs when interpretations of statutes change over time is that the meaning of statutory provisions can actually change. On some occasions, however, a court may conceive itself as deferring to a possibly mistaken decision about meaning, rather than accepting a change in meaning. On some other occasions, judges may rightly see themselves as departing from a provision's meaning. They should be candid about their understandings; they should not imply that they believe in a constancy of meaning that they do not in fact accept.

*

CHAPTER XX

THE MULTIPLE STRANDS OF INTERPRETATION AND HOW THEY MAY VARY

In proposing multiple standards for interpretation, I have rejected any proposal that interpretation "finally" comes down to any one criterion, such as an ordinary reading of the text or legislative intent. Statutory interpretation is, and should be, what William Eskridge has called "polycentric."[350] Exactly which proposed strands of interpretation should count for how much depends on a complex assessment that cannot be reduced to formulaic terms, except perhaps in such generalities as "a judge should interpret in accord with principles that best enhance desirable values within the legal system." On various issues, people can reasonably argue that approaches to interpreting meaning should be circumscribed in the interests of making judgments about statutes as simple and uniform as possible, but the judicial exercise is inevitably one of practical reason.[351]

350. Eskridge, *supra* note 84, at 55–56, 112.

351. Farber, *supra* note 189. *See* William Eskridge and Philip Frickey, "Statutory Interpretation as Practical Reasoning," 42 STAN. L. REV. 321 (1990). Nicholas Zeppos concludes, based on a study of sources cited in Supreme Court cases, that the Court's

The book as a whole allows us to revisit Questions 17–20 with added sophistication. We can see more fully why the best answers for one system may not be the best answers for all systems, and why the best answers for a system at one time may not be the best answers for it at another time. Let me restate those points in connection with legislative history.

As the legislative process changes, so also does the weight that should be given particular pieces of legislative history; it is possible that the process could change so much that reliance on legislative history, though once justified, would no longer be so. It has often been noted that, in some other common law countries, notably Great Britain, judges do not rely on legislative history (though the House of Lords has recently allowed consultation of legislative history in limited contexts).[352] In that country, a professional staff drafts legislation in close consultation with members of the government; as a consequence, language is much more carefully drafted and consistent in usage than in the United States. Further, because of party loyalty, bills proposed by the government get adopted in a form very close to that in which they are presented; language is not altered in unexpected ways. Courts can take

approach is eclectic, considering practical consequences and public values, as well as originalist sources, in "The Use of Authority in Statutory Interpretation: An Empirical Analysis," 70 Tex. L. Rev. 1073 (1992).

352.   Pepper v. Hart (1993) 1 All E.R. 42, 3 W.L.R. 1032. *See* T. St. J. N. Bates, "The Contemporary Use of Legislative History in the United Kingdom," 54 Cambridge L. J. 127 (1995).

the statutory language as a highly reliable guide to the goals a law is designed to accomplish; and judges are drawn from a narrow class of barristers who are well familiar with statutory language. These conditions are very different from those that exist in the United States, but the United States could change in the ways in which its laws are drafted and adopted.

Any practical analysis of the way in which judges should interpret statutes must straddle a difficult line that characterizes all recommendations about legal interpretation. To a large extent, judges are constrained to the existing conventions of a legal system, although there may be reason for movement in some direction. At present, the place of legislative history is sharply disputed among U.S. Supreme Court justices, and one can reasonably recommend a number of positions about that. But suppose that, for the last fifty years, all the justices had engaged in active and substantial use of legislative history. One could not responsibly recommend that its use be stopped forthwith, even if one thought the system would work better if our judges took the British approach. One could reasonably propose a steady diminution of reliance on legislative history, leading eventually to disuse.

In this book, I have not concentrated on how well my suggestions fit the dominant practice of judges—though at all points I believe my positions have substantial support in practice. Were a scholar or a judge to ask whether judges in any particular jurisdiction should now follow various suggestions, he would need to study connections to present practice in greater detail.

Like many social endeavors, statutory interpretation is complex. The book has analyzed major factors that judges take into account. Agreement about what counts in statutory interpretation, in particular the centrality of the text, is greater than one might suppose from surveying contesting theories. With respect to some matters, especially legislative intent, courts have understandably shied from trying to delve into the full logic of what they are doing. Many questions about statutory interpretation raise deep issues about our form of government and the respective roles of legislatures, courts, and administrative agencies. Although I have indicated some of my own perspectives, I have not offered definitive resolutions of these issues. It is genuine disagreements over these issues that trigger contending approaches to statutory meaning. Despite these disagreements, much about statutory interpretation is solidly established, both in practice and in theory.

Table of Cases

References are to Pages

285

*

INDEX

References Are to Pages

DRAFTING OF LEGISLATION—Cont'd
Model statutes, 156
Omitted words,, 46
Open-ended terms, intentional inclusion of in legislation, 228
Professionally drawn vs thrown together statutes, 14
Slips

generally, 45 et seq.
apparent textual meaning vs, 65 et seq.
arguments, slip, special status of, 65n
clear implications of text vs, 47 et seq.
purpose and, 66
Unjust results as evidence of drafting slip, 52n
Wasted drafting, 183

DWORKIN, RONALD
Generally, 11, 13, 17, 67, 118–119, 133, 146, 158, 172, 173, 192, 255

DYNAMIC INTERPRETATION
See PostEnactment Events (this index)

EASTERBROOK, FRANK
Generally, 51, 107, 137, 219, 221, 222, 259

ENDS AND MEANS
Conflicts between, 130

ERRORS
See Drafting of Legislation (this index)

ESKRIDGE, WILLIAM
Generally, 47, 67, 69–70, 127, 133, 135, 174–175, 201, 209–210, 224, 227, 229, 257–259, 262, 277, 281

EVALUATIVE JUDGMENTS
Necessity of, 9

EVOLUTIONISM
See also Change Over Time (this index); Post–Enactment Events (this index)
Originalists and evolutionists, debate between, 232

EXECUTIVE BRANCH
See also Administrative Agencies (this index)
Intentions of as bearing on legislative intent, 154 et seq.